Hard Press

THE QUEST

BY PO BAROJA

Contents

PART TWO

PART THREE

PART ONE

CHAPTER I

Preamble—Somewhat Immoral Notions of a Boarding-House Keeper—A
Balcony Is Heard Closing—A Cricket Chirps.

The clock in the corridor had just struck twelve, in a leisurely, rhythmic, decorous
manner. It was the habit of that tall old narrow-cased clock to accelerate or retard,
after its own sweet taste and whim, the uniform and monotonous series of hours that
encircle our life until it wraps it and leaves it, like an infant in its crib, in the obscure
bosom of time.

Soon after this friendly indication of the old clock, uttered in a solemn, peaceful
voice becoming an aged person, the hour of eleven rang out in a shrill, grotesque
fashion, with juvenile impertinence, from a petulant little clock of the vicinity, and a
few minutes later, to add to the confusion and the chronometric disorder, the bell of a
neighbouring church gave a single long, sonorous stroke that quivered for several
seconds in the silent atmosphere.

Which of the three clocks was correct? Which of those three devices for the
mensuration of time was the most exact in its indications?

The author cannot say, and he regrets it. He, regrets it, because Time, according to
certain solemn philosophers, is the canvas background against which we embroider
the follies of our existence, and truly it is little scientific not to be able to indicate at
precisely which moment the canvas of this book begins. But the author does not
know; all he can say is, that at that moment the steeds of night had for an appreciable
time been coursing across the heavens. It was, then, the hour of mystery; the hour
when wicked folk stalk abroad; the hour in which the poet dreams of immortality,
rhyming *hijos* with *prolijos* and *amor* with *dolor*; the hour in which the night-walker
slinks forth from her lair and the gambler enters his; the hour of adventures that are
sought and never found; the hour, finally, of the chaste virgin's dreams and of the
venerable old man's rheumatism. And as this romantic hour glided on, the shouts
and songs and quarrels of the street subsided; the lights in the balconies were
extinguished; the shopkeepers and janitors drew in their chairs from the gutter to
surrender themselves to the arms of sleep.

In the chaste, pure dwelling of Doa Casiana the boarding-house keeper, idyllic
silence had reigned for some time. Only through the balcony windows, which were
wide open, came the distant rumbling of carriages and the song of a neighbouring
cricket who scratched with disagreeable persistency upon the strident string of his
instrument.

At the hour, whatever it was, that was marked by the twelve slow, raucous snores of
the corridor clock, there were in the house only an old gentleman,—an impenitent
early-riser; the proprietress, Doa Casiana,—a landlady equally impenitent, to the
misfortune of her boarders, and the servant Petra.

At this moment the landlady was asleep, seated upon the rocking-chair before the open balcony; Petra, in the kitchen, was likewise asleep, with her head resting against the window-frame, while the old early-rising gentleman amused himself by coughing in bed.

Petra had finished scouring and her drowsiness, the heat and fatigue had doubtless overcome her. She could be made out dimly in the light of the small lamp that hung by the hearth. She was a thin, scrawny woman, flat-chested, with lean arms, big red hands and skin of greyish hue. She slept seated upon a chair with her mouth open; her breathing was short and laboured.

At the strokes of the corridor clock she suddenly awoke; she shut the window, through which came a nauseating, stable-like odour from the milk-dairy on the ground-floor; she folded the clothes and left with a pile of dishes, depositing them upon the dining-room table; then she laid away in a closet the table-ware, the tablecloth and the left-over bread; she took down the lamp and entered the room in the balcony of which the landlady sat sleeping.

"Seora, seora!" she called, several times.

"Eh? What is it?" murmured Doa Casiana drowsily.

"Perhaps you wish something?"

"No, nothing. Oh, yes! Tell the baker tomorrow that I'll pay him the coming Monday."

"Very well. Good-night."

The servant was leaving the room, when the balconies of the house across the way lighted up. They opened wide and soon there came the strains of a tender prelude from a guitar.

"Petra! Petra!" cried Doa Casiana. "Come here. Eh? Over in that Isabel's house ... You can tell they have visitors."

The domestic went to the balcony and gazed indifferently at the house opposite.

"Now that's what pays," the landlady went on. "Not this nasty boarding-house business."

At this juncture there appeared in one of the balconies of the other house a woman wrapped in a flowing gown, with a red flower in her hair. A young man in evening dress, with swallow-tail coat and white vest, clasped her tightly about the waist.

"That's what pays," repeated the landlady several times.

This notion must have stirred her ill-humour, for she added in an irritated voice:

"Tomorrow I'll have some plain words with that priest and those gadabout daughters of Doa Violante, and all the rest who are behind in their payments. To think a woman should have to deal with such a tribe! No! They'll laugh no more at me! ..."

Petra, without offering a reply, said good-night again and left the room. Doa Casiana continued to grumble, then ensconced her rotund person in the rocker and dozed off into a dream about an establishment of the same type as that across the way; but a model establishment, with luxuriously appointed salons, whither trooped in a long procession all the scrofulous youths of the clubs and fraternities, mystic and mundane, in such numbers that she was compelled to install a ticket-office at the entrance.

While the landlady lulled her fancy in this sweet vision of a brothel *de luxe*, Petra entered a dingy little room that was cluttered with old furniture. She set the light upon a chair, and placed a greasy box of matches on the top of the container; she read for a moment out of a filthy, begrimed devotionary printed in large type; she repeated several prayers with her eyes raised to the ceiling, then began to undress. The night was stifling; in that hole the heat was horrible. Petra got into bed, crossed herself, put out the lamp, which smoked for a long time, stretched herself out and laid her head upon the pillow. A worm in one of the pieces of furniture made the wood crack at regular intervals.

Petra slept soundly for a couple of hours, then awoke stifling from the heat. Somebody had just opened the door and footsteps were heard in the entry.

"That's Doa Violante and her daughters," mumbled Petra. "It must be pretty late."

The three women were probably returning from los Jardines, after having supped in search of the pesetas necessary to existence. Luck must have withheld its favour, for they were in bad humour and the two young women were quarrelling, each blaming the other for having wasted the night.

There were a number of venomous, ironic phrases, then the dispute ceased and silence was restored. Petra, thus kept awake, sank into her own thoughts; again footfalls were heard in the corridor, this time light and rapid. Then came the rasping of the shutter-bolt of a balcony that was being opened cautiously.

"One of them has got up," thought Petra. "What can the fuss be now?"

In a few minutes the voice of the landlady was heard shouting imperiously from her room:

10

"Irene! ... Irene!"

"Well?"

"Come in from the balcony."

"And why do I got to come in?" replied a harsh voice in rough, ill-pronounced accents.

"Because you must ... That's why."

"Why, what am I doing in the balcony?"

"That's something you know better than I."

"Well, I don't know."

"Well, I do."

"I was taking the fresh air."

"I guess you're fresh enough."

"You mean you are, seora."

"Close the balcony. You imagine that this house is something else."

"I? What have I done?"

"I don't have to tell you. For that sort of thing there's the house across the way, across the way."

"She means Isabel's," thought Petra.

The balcony was heard to shut suddenly; steps echoed in the entry, followed by the slamming of a door. For a long time the landlady continued her grumbling; soon came the murmuring of a conversation carried on in low tones. Then nothing more was heard save the persistent shrilling of the neighbouring cricket, who continued to scrape away at his disagreeable instrument with the determination of a beginner on the violin.

CHAPTER II

Doa Casiana's House—A Morning Ceremony—Conspiracy—Wherein Is
Discussed the Nutritive Value of Bones—Petra and her
Family—Manuel; his arrival in Madrid.

... And the cricket, now like an obstinate virtuoso, persisted in his musical exercises, which were truly somewhat monotonous, until the sky was brightened by the placid smile of dawn. At the very first rays of the sun the performer relented, doubtless content with the perfection of his artistic efforts, and a quail took up his solo, giving the three regulation strokes. The watchman knocked with his pike at the stores, one or two bakers passed with their bread, a shop was opened, then another, then a vestibule; a servant threw some refuse out on the sidewalk, a newsboy's calling was heard.

The author would be too bold if he tried to demonstrate the mathematical necessity imposed upon Doa Casiana's house of being situated on Mesonero Romanos Street rather than upon Olivo, for, undoubtedly, with the same reason it might have been placed upon Desengao, Tudescos or any other thoroughfare. But the duties of the author, his obligation as an impartial and veracious chronicler compel him to speak the truth, and the truth is that the house was on Mesonero Romanos Street rather than on Olivo.

At this early hour not a sound could be heard inside; the janitor had opened the vestibule-entrance and was regarding the street with a certain melancholy.

The vestibule,—long, dingy, and ill-smelling,—was really a narrow corridor, at one side of which was the janitor's lodge.

On passing this lodge, if you glanced inside, where it was encumbered with furniture till no room was left, you could always make out a fat woman, motionless, very swarthy, in whose arms reposed a pale weakling of a child, long and thin, like a white earthworm. It seemed that above the window, instead of "Janitor" the legend should have read: "The Woman-Cannon and her Child," or some similar sign from the circus tents.

If any question were addressed to this voluminous female she would answer in a shrill voice accompanied by a rather disagreeable gesture of disdain. Leaving the den of this woman-cannon to one side, you would proceed; at the left of the entrance began the staircase, always in darkness, with no air except what filtered in through a few high, grated windows that opened upon a diminutive courtyard with filthy walls punctured by round ventilators. For a broad, roomy nose endowed with a keen pituitary membrane, it would have been a curious sport to discover and investigate the provenience and the species of all the vile odours comprising that fetid stench, which was an inalienable characteristic of the establishment.

12

The author never succeeded in making the acquaintance of the persons living upon the upper floors. He has a vague notion that there were two or three landladies, a family who let out rooms to permanent gentlemen boarders, but nothing else. Wherefore the author does not climb those heights but pauses upon the first landing.

Here, at least by day, could be made out in the reigning darkness, a tiny door; at night, on the other hand, by the light of a kerosene lantern one could glimpse a tin door-plate painted red, upon which was inscribed in black letters: "Casiana Fernndez."

At one side of the door hung a length of blackish rusted chain that could be reached only by standing on tiptoe and stretching out one's arm; but as the door was always ajar, the lodgers could come and go without the need of knocking.

This led to the house. By day, one was plunged into utter obscurity; the sole thing that indicated a change of place was the smell, not so much because it was more agreeable than that of the staircase, as because it was distinct; on the contrary, at night, in the vague light shed by a cork night-taper afloat in the water and oil of a bowl that was attached to the wall by a brass ring, there could be seen through a certain dim nebulosity, the furniture, the pictures and the other paraphernalia that occupied the reception hall.

Facing the entrance stood a broad, solid table on which reposed an old-fashioned music-box consisting of several cylinders that bristled with pins; close beside it, a plaster statue: a begrimed figure lacking a nose, and difficult to distinguish as some god, half-god or mortal.

On the wall of the reception room and of the corridor hung some large, indistinct oil paintings. A person of intelligence would perhaps have considered them detestable, but the landlady, who imagined that a very obscure painting must be very good, refreshed herself betimes with the thought that mayhap these pictures, sold to an Englishman, would, one day make her independent.

There were several canvases in which the artist had depicted horrifying biblical scenes: massacres, devastation, revolting plagues; but all this in such a manner, that, despite the painter's lavish distribution of blood, wounds and severed heads, these canvases instead of horrifying, produced an impression of merriment. One of them represented the daughter of Herodias contemplating the head of St. John the Baptist. Every figure expressed amiable joviality: the monarch, with the indumentary of a card-pack king and in the posture of a card-player, was smiling; his daughter, a florid-face dame, was smiling; the familiars, encased in their huge helmets, were smiling, and the very head of St. John the Baptist was smiling from its place upon a repouss platter. Doubtless the artist of these paintings, if he lacked the gift of design and colour, was endowed with that of joviality.

To the right and left of the house door ran the corridor, from whose walls hung another exhibit of black canvases, most of them unframed, in which could be made out absolutely nothing; only in one of them, after very patient scrutiny, one might guess at a red cock pecking at the leaves of a green cabbage.

Upon this corridor opened the bedrooms, in which, until very late in the afternoon, dirty socks and torn slippers were usually seen strewn upon the floor, while on the unmade beds lay collars and cuffs.

Almost all the boarders in that house got up late, except two travelling salesmen, a bookkeeper and a priest, who arose early through love of their occupations, and an old gentleman who did so through habit or for reasons of hygiene.

The bookkeeper would be off, without breakfast, at eight in the morning; the priest left *in albis* to say mass; but the salesmen had the audacious presumption to eat a bite in the house, and the landlady resorted to a very simple procedure to send them off without so much as a sip of water; these two agents began work between half-past nine and ten; they retired very late, bidding their landlady wake them at eight-thirty. She would see to it that they were not aroused until ten. When they awoke and saw the time, they would jump out of bed, hurriedly dress and dash off like a shot, cursing the landlady. Then, when the feminine element of the house gave signs of life, every nook would echo with cries, discordant voices, conversations shouted from one bedchamber to another, and out of the rooms, their hands armed with the night-service, would come the landlady, one of Doa Violante's daughters, a tall, obese Biscayan Lady, and another woman whom they called the Baroness.

The landlady invariably wore a corset-cover of yellow flannel, the Baroness a wrapper mottled with stains from cosmetics and the Biscayan lady a red waist through whose opening was regularly presented, for the admiration of those who happened along the corridor, a huge white udder streaked with coarse blue veins.

After this matutinal ceremony, and not infrequently during the same, complaints, disputes, gossip and strife would arise, providing tid-bits for the remaining hours.

On the day following the scrape between the landlady and Irene, when the latter returned to her room after having fulfilled her mission, a secret conclave was held by those who remained.

"Don't you know? Didn't you hear anything last night?" asked the Biscayan.

"No," replied the landlady and the Baroness. "What happened?"

"Irene smuggled a man into the house last night."

"She did?"

"I heard her talking to him myself."

14

"And he must have opened the street door! The dog!" muttered the landlady.

"No; the man came from this tenement."

"One of the students from upstairs," offered the Baroness.

"I'll tell a thing or two to the rascally fellow," replied Doa Casiana.

"No. Take your time," answered the Biscayan. "We're going to give her and her gallant a fright. If he comes tonight, while they're talking, we'll tell the watchman to knock at the house door, and at the same time we'll all come out of our rooms with lights, as if we were going to the dining-room, and catch them."

While this plot was being hatched in the corridor, Petra was preparing breakfast in the obscurity of the kitchen. There was very little to prepare, for the meal invariably consisted of a fried egg, which never by any accident was large, and a beefsteak, which, in memories reverting to the remotest epoch, had not a single time by any exception been soft.

At noon, the Biscayan, in tones of deep mystery, told Petra about the conspiracy, but the maid-of-all-work was in no mood for jests that day. She had just received a letter that filled her with worriment. Her brother-in-law wrote her that Manuel, the eldest of Petra's children, was being sent to Madrid. No lucid explanation of the reason for this decision was given. The letter stated simply that back there in the village the boy was only wasting his time, and that it would be better for him to go to Madrid and learn a trade.

This letter had set Petra thinking. After wiping the dishes, she washed herself in the kneeding-trough; she could not shake the fixed idea that if her brother-in-law was sending Manuel to her it was because the boy had been up to some mischief. She would soon find out, for he was due to arrive that night.

Petra had four children, two boys and two girls; the girls were well placed; the elder as a maid, with some very wealthy religious ladies, the younger in a government official's home.

The boys gave her more bother; the younger not so much, since, as they said, he continued to reveal a steady nature. The elder, however, was rebellious and intractable.

"He doesn't take after me," thought Petra. "In fact, he's quite like my husband."

And this disquieted her. Her husband, Manuel Alczar, had been an energetic, powerful man, and, towards his last days, harsh-tempered and brutal.

He was a locomotive machinist and earned good pay. Petra and he could not get along together and the couple were always at blows.

Folks and friends alike blamed Alczar the machinist for everything, as if the systematic contrariness of Petra, who seemed to enjoy nagging the man, were not enough to exasperate any one. Petra had always been that way,—wilful, behind the mask of humility, and as obstinate as a mule. As long as she could do as she pleased the rest mattered little.

While the machinist was alive, the family's economic situation had been relatively comfortable. Alczar and Petra paid sixteen duros per month for their rooms on Relojo street, and took in boarders: a mail clerk and other railroad employs.

Their domestic existence might have been peaceful and pleasureful were it not for the daily altercations between husband and wife. They had both come to feel such a need for quarrelling that the most insignificant cause would lead to scandalous scenes. It was enough that he said white for her to cry black; this opposition infuriated the machinist, who would throw the dishes about, belabour his wife, and smash all the household furniture. Then Petra, satisfied that she had sufficient cause for affliction, shut herself in her room to weep and pray.

What with his alcohol, his fits of temper, and his hard work, the machinist went about half dazed; on one terribly hot day in August he fell from the train on to the roadbed and was found dead without a wound.

Petra, disregarding the advice of her boarders, insisted upon changing residence, as she disliked that section of the city. This she did, taking in new lodgers—unreliable, indigent folk who ran up large bills or never paid at all—and in a short time she found herself compelled to sell her furniture and abandon her new house.

Then she hired out her daughters as servants, sent her two boys off to a little town in the province of Soria, where her brother-in-law was the superintendent of a small railway station, and herself entered as a domestic in Doa Casiana's lodging-house. Thus she descended from mistress to servant, without complaint. It was enough that the idea had occurred to her; therefore it was best.

She had been there for two years, saving her pay. Her ambition was to have her sons study in a seminary and graduate as priests. And now came the return of Manuel, the elder son, to upset her plans. What could have happened?

She made various conjectures. In the meantime with her deformed hands she removed the lodgers' dirty laundry. In through the courtyard window wafted a confusion of songs and disputing voices, alternating with the screech of the clothes-line pulleys.

In the middle of the afternoon Petra began preparation for dinner. The mistress ordered every morning a huge quantity of bones for the sustenance of her boarders. It is very possible that there was, in all that heap of bones, a Christian one from time to time; certainly, whether they came from carnivorous animals or from ruminants, there was rarely on those tibiae, humeri, and femora a tiny scrap of meat. The ossuary boiled away in the huge pot with beans that had been tempered with bicarbonate, and with the broth was made the soup, which, thanks to its quantity of fat, seemed like some turbid concoction for cleaning glassware or polishing gilt.

After inspecting the state of the ossuary in the stew-pot, Petra made the soup, and then set about extracting all the scrap meat from the bones and covering them hypocritically with a tomato sauce. This was the *pice de rsistance* in Doa Casiana's establishment.

Thanks to this hygienic regimen, none of the boarders fell ill with obesity, gout or any of those other ailments due to excess of food and so frequent in the rich.

After preparing the meal and serving it, Petra postponed the dish-washing, and left the house to meet her son.

Night had not yet fallen. The sky was vaguely red, the air stifling, heavy with a dense mist of dust and steam. Petra went up Carretas Street, continued through Atocha, entered the Estacin del Medioda and sat down on a bench to wait for Manuel....

Meanwhile, the boy was approaching the city half asleep, half asphyxiated, in a third-class compartment.

He had taken the train the night before at the railway station where his uncle was superintendent. On reaching Almazn, he had to wait more than an hour for a mixed train, so he sauntered through the deserted streets to kill time.

To Manuel, Almazn seemed vast, infinitely sad; the town, glimpsed through the gloom of a dimly starlit night, loomed like a great, fanastic, dead city. The pale electric lights shone upon its narrow streets and low houses; the spacious plaza with its arc lights was deserted; the belfry of a church rose into the heavens.

Manuel strolled down towards the river. From the bridge the town seemed more fantastic and mysterious than ever; upon a wall might be made out the galleries of a palace, and several lofty, sombre towers shot up from amidst the jumbled dwellings of the town; a strip of moon gleamed close to the horizon, and the river, divided by a few islets into arms, glittered as if it were mercury.

Manuel left Almaznhad to wait a few hours in Alcuneza for the next train. He was weary, and as there were no benches in the station, he stretched himself out upon the floor amidst bundles and skins of oil.

At dawn he boarded the other train, and despite the hardness of the seat, managed to fall asleep.

Manuel had been two years with his relatives; he departed from their home with more satisfaction than regret.

Life had held no pleasure for him during those two years.

The tiny station presided over by his uncle was near a poor hamlet surrounded by arid, stony tracts upon which grew neither tree nor bush. A Siberian temperature reigned in those parts, but the inclemencies of Nature were nothing to bother a little boy, and gave Manuel not the slightest concern.

The worst of it all was that neither his uncle nor his uncle's wife showed any affection for him, rather indifference, and this indifference prepared the boy to receive their few benefactions with utter coldness.

It was different with Manuel's brother, to whom the couple gradually took a liking.

The two youngsters displayed traits almost absolutely opposite; the elder, Manuel, was of a frivolous, slothful, indolent disposition, and would neither study nor go to school. He was fond of romping about the fields and engaging in bold, dangerous escapades. The characteristic trait of Juan, the younger brother, was a morbid sentimentalism that would overflow in tears upon the slightest provocation.

Manuel recalled that the school master and town organist, an old fellow who was half dominie and taught the two brothers Latin, had always prophesied that Juan would make his mark; Manuel he considered as an adventure-seeking rover who would come to a bad end.

As Manuel dozed in the third-class compartment, a thousand recollections thronged his imagination: the events of the night before at his uncle's mingled in his mind with fleeting impressions of Madrid already half forgotten. One by one the sensations of distinct epochs intertwined themselves in his memory, without rhyme or reason and among them, in the phantasmagoria of near and distant images that rolled past his inner vision, there stood out clearly those sombre towers glimpsed by night in Almazn by the light of the moon....

When one of his travelling companions announced that they had already reached Madrid, Manuel was filled with genuine anxiety. A red dusk flushed the sky, which was streaked with blood like some monster's eye; the train gradually slackened speed; it glided through squalid suburbs and past wretched houses; by this time, the electric lights were gleaming pallidly above the high signal lanterns....

The train rolled on between long lines of coaches, the round-tables trembled with an iron rumble, and the Estacin del Medioda, illuminated by arc lamps, came into view.

18

The travellers got out; Manuel descended with his little bundle of clothes in his hand, looked in every direction for a glimpse of his mother and could not make her out anywhere on the wide platform. For a moment he was confused, then decided to follow the throng that was hurrying with bundles and bird-cages toward a gate; he was asked for his ticket, he stopped to go through his pockets, found it and issued into the street between two rows of porters who were yelling the names of hotels.

"Manuel! Where are you going?"

There was his mother. Petra had meant to be severe; but at the sight of her son she forgot her severity and embraced him effusively.

"But—what happened?" Petra asked at once.

"Nothing."

"Then—why have you come?"

"They asked me whether I wanted to stay there or go to Madrid, and I said I'd rather go to Madrid."

"Nothing more?"

"Nothing more," replied Manuel simply.

"And Juan? Was he studying?"

"Yes. Much more than I was. Is the house far off, Mother?"

"Yes, Why? Are you hungry?"

"I should say. I haven't had a bite all the way."

They left the Station at the Prado; then they walked up Alcal street. A dusty mist quivered in the air; the street-lamp shone opaquely in the turbid atmosphere.... As soon as they reached the house Petra made supper for Manuel and prepared a bed for him upon the floor, beside her own. The youth lay down, but so violent was the contrast between the hamlet's silence and the racket of footsteps, conversations and cries that resounded through the house, that, despite his weariness, Manuel could not sleep.

He heard every lodger come in; it was past midnight when the disturbance quieted down; suddenly a squabble burst out followed by a crash of laughter which ended in a triply blasphemous imprecation and a slap that woke the echoes.

"What can that be, Mother?" asked Manuel from his bed.

"That's Doa Violante's daughter whom they've caught with her sweetheart," Petra answered, half from her sleep. Then it occurred to her that it was imprudent to tell this to her boy, and she added, gruffly:

"Shut up and go to sleep."

The music-box in the reception-room, set going by the hand of one of the boarders, commenced to tinkle that sentimental air from *La Mascotte*,—the duet between Pippo and Bettina:

Will you forget me, gentle swain?

Then all was silent.

CHAPTER III

First Impressions of Madrid—The Boarders—Idyll—Sweet and
Delightful Lessons.

Manuel's mother had a relation, her husband's cousin, who was a cobbler. Petra had decided, some days previously, to give Manuel into apprenticeship at the shoe-shop; but she still hoped the boy would be convinced that it was better for him to study something than to learn a trade, and this hope had deterred her from the resolution to send the boy to her relative's house.

Persuading the landlady to permit Manuel to remain in the house cost Petra no little labour, but at last she succeeded. It was agreed that the boy would run errands and help to serve meals. Then when the vacation season had passed, he would resume his studies.

On the day following his arrival the youngster assisted his mother at the table.

All the borders, except the Baroness and her girl, were seated in the dining-room, presided over by the landlady with her wrinkle-fretted, parchment-hued face and its thirty-odd moles.

The dining-room, a long, narrow habitation with a window opening on the courtyard, communicated with two narrow corridors that switched off at right angles; facing the window stood a dark walnut sideboard whose shelves were laden with porcelain, glassware and cups and glasses in a row. The centre table was so large for such a small room that when the boarders were seated it scarcely left space for passage at the ends.

The yellow wall-paper, torn in many spots, displayed, at intervals, grimy circles from the oil of the lodgers' hair; reclining in their seats they would rest the back of the chairs and their heads against the wall.

The furniture, the straw chairs, the paintings, the mat full of holes,—everything in that room was filthy, as if the dust of many years had settled upon the articles and clung to the sweat of several generations of lodgers.

By day the dining-room was dark; by night it was lighted by a flickering kerosene lamp that smudged the ceiling with smoke.

The first time that Manuel, following his mother's instructions, served at table, the landlady, as usual, presided. At her right sat an old gentleman of cadaverous aspect,—a very fastidious personage who conscientiously wiped the glasses and plates with his napkin. By his side this gentleman had a vial and a dropper, and before eating he would drop his medicine into the wine. To the left of the landlady rose the Biscayan, a tall, stout woman of bestial appearance, with a huge nose, thick lips and flaming cheeks; next to this lady, as flat as a toad, was Doa Violante, whom the boarders jestingly called now Doa Violent and now Doa Violated.

Near Doa Violante were grouped her daughters; then a priest who prattled incessantly, a journalist whom they called the Superman,—a very fair youth, exceedingly thin and exceedingly serious,—the salesmen and the bookkeeper.

Manuel served the soup and all the boarders took it, sipping it with a disagreeable inhalation. Then, according to his mother's orders, the youngster remained standing there. Now followed the beans which, if not for their size then for their hardness might have figured in an artillery park, and one of the boarders permitted himself some pleasantry about the edibleness of so petreous a vegetable; a pleasantry that glided over the impassive countenance of Doa Casiana without leaving the slightest trace.

Manuel sat about observing the boarders. It was the day after the conspiracy; Doa Violante and her daughters were incommunicative and in ugly humour. Doa Violante's inflated face at every moment creased into a frown, and her restless, turbid eyes betrayed deep preoccupation. Celia, the elder of the daughters, annoyed by the priest's jests, began to answer violently, cursing everything human and divine with a desperate, picturesque, raging hatred, which caused loud, universal laughter. Irene, the culprit of the previous night's scandal, a girl of some fifteen or sixteen years with a broad head, large hands and feet, an as yet incompletely developed body and heavy, ungainly movements, spoke scarcely a word and kept her gaze fixed upon her plate.

The meal at an end, the lodgers went off to their various tasks. At night Manuel served supper without dropping a thing or making a single mistake, but in five or six days he was forever doing things wrong.

It is impossible to judge how much of an impression was made upon the boy by the usage and customs of the boarding roost and the species of birds that inhabited it; but they could not have impressed him much. Manuel, while he served at table in the days that followed, had to put up with and endless succession of remarks, jests and practical jokes.

A thousand incidents, comical enough to one who did not have to suffer them, turned up at every step; now they would discover tobacco in the soup, now coal, ashes, and shreds of coloured paper in the water-bottle.

One of the salesmen, who was troubled with his stomach and spent his days gazing at the reflection of his tongue in the mirror, would jump up in fury when one of these jokes was perpetrated, and ask the proprietress to discharge an incompetent booby who committed such atrocities.

Manuel grew accustomed to these manifestations against his humble person, and when they scolded him he retorted with the most bare-faced impudence and indifference.

Soon he learned the life and miracles of every boarder and was ready to talk back in outrageous fashion if they tried his patience.

Doa Violante and her daughters,—especially the old lady, showed a great liking for the boy. The three women had now been living in the house for several months; they paid little and when they couldn't pay at all, they didn't. But they were easily satisfied. All three occupied an inner room that opened onto the courtyard, whence came a nauseating odour of fermented milk that escaped from the stable of the ground floor.

The hole in which they lived was not large enough to move about in; the room assigned to them by the landlady—in proportion to the size of their rent and the insecurity of the payment—was a dark den occupied by two narrow iron beds, between which, in the little space left, was crammed a cot.

Here slept these gallant dames; by day they scoured all Madrid, and spent their existence making arrangements with money-lenders, pawning articles and taking them out of pawn.

The two young ladies, Celia and Irene, although they were mother and daughter, passed for sisters. Doa Violante, in her better days, had led the life of a petty courtesan and had succeeded in hoarding up a tidy bit as provision against the winter of old age, when a former patron convinced her that he had a remarkable combination for winning a fortune at the Fronton. Doa Violante fell into the trap and her patron left her without a cntimo. Then Doa Violante went back to the old life, became half blind and reached that lamentable state at which surely she would have arrived much sooner if, early in her career, she had developed a talent for living respectably.

The old lady passed most of the day in the confinement of her dark room, which reeked of stable odors, rice powder and cosmetics; at night she had to accompany her daughter and her granddaughter on walks, and to cafs and theatres, on the hunt and capture of the kid, as it was put by the travelling salesman who suffered from his stomach,—a fellow half humorist and half grouch. When they were in the house Celia and Irene, the daughter and the granddaughter of Doa Violante, kept bickering at all hours; perhaps this continuous state of irritation derived from the close quarters in which they lived; perhaps so much passing as sisters in the eyes of others had convinced them that they really were, so that they quarrelled and insulted one another as such.

The one point on which they agreed was that Doa Violante was in their way; the burden of the blind woman frightened away every libidinous old fellow that came within the range of Irene and Celia.

The landlady, Doa Casiana, who at the slightest occasion suspected the abandonment of the blind old woman, admonished the two maternally to gird themselves with patience; Doa Violante, after all, was not, like Calypso, immortal. But they replied that this toiling away at full speed just to keep the old lady in medicine and syrups wasn't at all to their taste.

Doa Casiana shook her head sadly, for her age and circumstances enabled her to put herself in Doa Violante's place, and she argued with this example, asking them to put themselves in the grandmother's position; but neither was convinced.

Then the landlady advised them to peer into her mirror. She—as she assured them—had descended from the heights of the Comandancia (her husband had been a commander of the carbineers) to the wretchedness of running a boarding-house, yet she was resigned, and her lips curled in a stoic smile.

Doa Casiana knew the meaning of resignation and her only solace in this life was a few volumes of novels in serial form, two or three feuilletons, and a murky liquid mysteriously concocted by her own hands out of sugared water and alcohol.

This beverage she poured into a square, wide-mouthed flask, into which she placed a thick stem of anis. She kept it in the closet of her bedroom.

Some one who discovered the flask with its black twig of anis compared it to those bottles in which fetuses and similar nasty objects are preserved, and since that time, whenever the landlady appeared with rosy cheeks, a thousand comments—not at all favourable to the madame's abstinence—ran from lodger to lodger.

"Doa Casiana's tipsy from her fetus-brandy."

"The good lady drinks too much of that fetus."

"The fetus has gone to her head...."

Manuel took a friendly part in this witty merriment of the boarders. The boy's faculties of adaptation were indisputably enormous, for after a week in the landlady's house it was as if he had always lived there.

His skill at magic was sharpened: whenever he was needed he was not to be seen and no sooner was anybody's back turned than he was in the street playing with the boys of the neighbourhood.

As a result of his games and his scrapes he got his clothes so dirty and torn that the landlady nicknamed him the page Don Rompe-Galas, recalling a tattered character from a sanete that Doa Casiana, according to her affirmations, had seen played in her halycon days.

24

Generally, those who most made use of Manuel's services were the journalist whom they called the Superman—he sent the boy off with copy to the printers—and Celia and Irene, who employed him for bearing notes and requests for money to their friends. Doa Violante, whenever she pilfered a few cntimos from her daughter would dispatch Manuel to the store for a package of cigarettes, and give him a cigar for the errand.

"Smoke it here," she would say. "Nobody'll see you."

Manuel would sit down upon a trunk and the old lady, a cigarette in her mouth and blowing smoke through her nostrils, would recount adventures from the days of her glory.

That room of Doa Violante and her daughters was a haunt of infection; from the hooks nailed to the wall hung dirty rags, and between the lack of air and the medley of odours a stench arose strong enough to fell an ox.

Manuel listened to Doa Violante's stories with genuine delight. The old lady was at her best in her commentaries.

"I tell you, my boy," she would say, "you can take my word for it. A woman with a good pair of breasts and who happens to be a pretty warm article"—and here the old lady pulled at her cigarette and with an expressive gesture indicated what she meant by her no less expressive word—"will always have a trail of men after her."

Doa Violante used to sing songs from Spanish *zarzuelas* and from French operettas, which produced in Manuel a terrible sadness. He could not say why, but they gave him the impression of a world of pleasures that was hopelessly beyond his reach. When he heard Doa Violante sing the song from *El Juramento*

Disdain is a sword with a double edge,
One slays with love, the other with forgetfulness....

he had a vision of salons, ladies, amorous intrigues; but even more than by this he was overwhelmed with sadness by the waltzes from *La Dina* and *La Grande Duchesse*.

Doa Violante's reflexions opened Manuel's eyes; the scenes that occurred daily in the house, however, worked quite as much as these toward such a result.

Another good instructor was found in the person of Doa Casiana's niece, a trifle older than Manuel,—a thin, weakly chit of such a malicious nature that she was always hatching plots against somebody.

If any one struck her she didn't shed a tear; she would go down to the concierge's lodge when the concierge's little boy was left alone, would grab him and pinch him and kick him, in this manner wreaking vengeance for the blows she had received.

After eating, almost all of the boarders went off to their affairs; Celia and Irene, together with the Biscayan, indulged in a grand frolic by spying upon the women in Isabel's house, who would come out on the balcony and chat, or signal to the neighbours. At times these miserable brothel odalisques were not content with speaking; they would dance and exhibit their calves.

Manuel's mother, as always, would be meditating upon heaven and hell, giving little heed to the pettiness of this earth, and she could not shield her son from such edifying spectacles. Petra's educational system consisted only of giving Manuel an occasional blow and of making him read prayer-books.

Petra imagined that she could see the traits of the machinist showing up in the boy, and this troubled her. She wished Manuel to be like her,—humble toward his superiors, respectful toward the priests...; but a fine place this was for learning to respect anything!

One morning, after the solemn ceremony had been celebrated in which all the women of the house issued into the corridor swinging their night service, there burst from Doa Violante's room a clamour of shouts, weeping, stamping and vociferation.

The landlady, the Biscayan and several of the boarders tiptoed into the corridor to pry. Inside the quarrellers must have realized that they were being spied upon, for they opened the door and the fray continued in low tones.

Manuel and the landlady's niece remained in the entry. They could hear Irene's sobbing and the scolding voices of Celia and Doa Violante.

At first they could not make out what was being said; but soon the three women forgot their determination to speak low and their voices rose in anger.

"Go! Go to the House of Mercy and have them rid you of that swelling! Wretch!" cried Celia.

"Well, what of it?" retorted Irene. "I'm caught, am I? I know it. What of it?"

Doa Violante opened the door to the entry furiously; Manuel and the landlady's niece scampered off, and the old lady came out in a patched flannel shift and a weed kerchief tied about her ears, and began to pace to and fro, dragging her worn-out shoes from end to end of the corridor.

"The sow! Worse than a sow!" she muttered. "Did any one ever see such a filthy creature!"

26

Manuel went off to the parlour, where the landlady and the Biscayan were chatting in low tones. The landlady's niece, dying with curiosity, questioned the two women with growing irritation:

"But why are they scolding Irene?"

The landlady and the Biscayan exchanged amicable glances and burst into laughter.

"Tell me," cried the child insistently, clutching at her aunt's kerchief. "What of it if she has that bundle? Who gave her that package?"

The landlady and the Biscayan could no longer restrain their guffaws, while the little girl stared avidly up at them, trying to make out the meaning of what she heard.

"Who gave her that package?" repeated the Biscayan between outbursts. "My dear little girl, we really don't know who gave her that package."

All the boarders repeated the niece's question with enthusiastic delight, and at every table discussion some wag would be sure to interrupt suddenly with:

"Now I see that you know who gave her that package." The remark would be greeted with uproarious merriment.

Then, after a few days had passed, there was rumour of a mysterious consultation held by Doa Violante's daughters with the wife of a barber on Jardines street,—a sort of provider of little angels for limbo; it was said that Irene returned from the conference in a coach, very pale, and that she had to be put at once to bed. Certainly the girl did not leave her room for more than a week and, when she appeared, she looked like a convalescent and the frowns had disappeared completely from the face of her mother and her grandmother.

"She looks like an infanticide," said the priest when he saw her again, "but she's prettier than ever."

Whether any transgression had been committed, none could say with surety; soon everything was forgotten; a patron appeared for the girl, and he was, from all appearances, wealthy. In commemoration of so happy an event the boarders participated in the treat. After the supper they drank cognac and brandy, the priest played the guitar, Irene danced *sevillanas* with less grace than a bricklayer, as the landlady said; the Superman sang some *fados* that he had learned in Portugal, and the Biscayan, not to be outdone, burst forth into some *malagueas* that might just as well have been a *cante flamenco* or the Psalms of David.

Only the blond student with the eyes of steel abstained from the celebration; he was absorbed in his thoughts.

"And you, Roberto," Celia said to him several times,—"don't you sing or do anything?"

"Not I," he replied coldly.

"You haven't any blood in your veins."

The youth looked at her for a moment, shrugged his shoulders indifferently and his pale lips traced a smile of disdainful mockery.

Then, as almost always happened in these boarding-house sprees, some wag turned on the music-box in the corridor and the duet from *La Mascotte* together with the waltz from *La Diva* rose in confusion upon the air; the Superman and Celia danced a couple of waltzes and the party wound up with everybody singing a *habanera*, until they wearied and each owl flew off to his nest.

CHAPTER IV

Oh, love, love!—What's Don Telmo Doing?—Who is Don
Telmo?—Wherein the Student and Don Telmo Assume Certain
Novelesque Proportions.

The Baroness was hardly ever seen in the house, except during the early hours of the morning and the night. She dined and supped outside. If the landlady was to be credited, she was an adventuress whose position varied considerably, for one day she would be moving to a costly apartment and sporting a carriage, while the next she would disappear for several months in the germ-ridden hole of some cheap boarding-house.

The Baroness's daughter, a child of some twelve or fourteen years, never appeared in the dining-room or in the corridor; her mother forbade all communication with the lodgers. Her name was Kate. She was a fair girl, very light-complexioned and exceedingly winsome. Only the student Roberto spoke to her now and then in English.

The youth was enthusiastic over her.

That summer the Baroness's streak of bad luck must have come to an end, for she began to make herself some fine clothes and prepared to move.

For several weeks a modiste and her assistant came daily, with gowns and hats for the Baroness and Kate.

Manuel, one night, saw the modiste's assistant go by with a huge box in her hand and was smitten.

He followed her at a distance in great fear lest she see him. As he stole on behind, he wondered what he could say to such a maiden if he were to accompany her. It must be something gallant, exquisite; he even imagined that she was at his side and he racked his brain for beautiful phrases and delicate compliments, yet nothing but commonplaces rewarded his search. In the meantime the assistant and her box were lost in the crowd and he could not catch sight of them again.

The memory of that maiden was for Manuel as an enchanting music, a fancy upon which were reared still wilder fancies. Often he made up tales in which always he figured as the hero and the assistant as the heroine. While Manuel bemoaned the harshness of fate, Roberto, the blond student, gave himself up likewise to melancholy, brooding upon the Baroness's daughter. The student was forced to endure jests especially from Celia, who, according to certain evil tongues, was trying to rouse him from his habitual frigidity. But Roberto gave her no heed.

Some days later the house was agog with curiosity.

As the boarders came in from the street, they greeted each other jokingly, repeating in the manner of a pass-word: "Who is Don Telmo? What's Don Telmo doing?"

One day the district police-commissioner came and spoke to Don Telmo, and some one heard or invented the report that the two men were discussing the notorious crime on Malasana Street. Upon hearing this news the expectant inquisitiveness of the boarders waxed great, and all, half in jest and half in earnest, arranged to keep a watch upon the mysterious gentleman.

Don Telmo was the name of the cadaverous old fellow who wiped his cups and spoons with his napkin, and his reserved manner seemed to invite observation. Taciturn, indifferent, never joining the conversation, a man of few words who never made any complaints, he attracted attention by the very fact that he seemed intent upon not attracting it.

His only visible occupation was to wind the seven or eight clocks of the house and to regulate them when they got out of order,—an event of common occurrence.

Don Telmo had the features of a very sad man,—one in profound sorrow. His livid countenance betrayed fathomless dejection. He wore his white beard and his hair short; his brows fell like brushes over his grey eyes.

In the house he went around wrapped in a faded coat, with a Greek bonnet and cloth slippers. When he went out he donned a long frock coat and a very tall silk hat; only on certain summer days would he wear a Havana hat of woven straw.

For more than a month Don Telmo was the topic of conversation in the boarding-house.

In the famous trial of the Malasana Street crime a servant declared that one afternoon she saw Doa Celsa's son in an aqueduct of the Plaza de Oriente, talking with a lame old man. For the guests this man could be none other than Don Telmo. With this suspicion they set about spying upon the old man; he, however, had a sharp scent and sniffed the state of affairs at once; the boarders, seeing how bootless their attempts were proving, tried to ransack his room; they used a number of keys until they got the door open and when they had forced an entrance, discovered nothing more that a closet fastened by a formidable safety-lock.

The Biscayan and Roberto, the blond student, opposed this campaign of espionage. The Superman, the priest, the salesmen and the women of the establishment made up that the Biscayan and the student were allies of Don Telmo, and, in all probability, accomplices in the Malasana Street crime.

"Without a doubt," averred the Superman, "Don Telmo killed Doa Celsa Nebot; the Biscayan poured oil over the body and set it afire, and Roberto hid the jewels in the house on Amaniel Street."

"That cold bird!" replied Celia. "What could he do?"

"Nothing, nothing. We must keep on their track," said the curate.

"And get some money out of that old Shylock," added the Superman.

This espionage, carried on half in joke and half in all seriousness, wound up in debates and disputes, and as a result two groups were formed in the house; that of the Sensible folk, comprised by the three criminals and the landlady, and that of the Foolish, in which were enrolled all the rest.

This limitation of sides forced Roberto and Don Telmo into intimacy, so that the student changed his place at the table and sat next to the old man.

One night, after eating, while Manuel was removing the service, the plates and the cups, Don Telmo and Roberto were engaged in conversation.

The student was a dogmatic reasoner, dry, rectilinear, never swerving from his point of view; he spoke but little, but when he did speak, it was in a sententious manner.

One day, discussing whether or not young men should be ambitious and look to the future, Roberto asserted that the first was the proper course.

"Well, that isn't what you're doing," commented the Superman.

"I am absolutely convinced," replied Roberto, "that some day I'm going to be a millionaire. I am engaged in constructing the machinery that will bring me a fortune."

The Superman posed as a man of the world who had seen many things; upon hearing this he permitted himself a scoffing remark concerning Roberto's ability, and the youth retorted in so violent and aggressive a manner that the journalist lost his composure and blurted out a string of apologies.

Afterwards, when Don Telmo and Roberto were left alone at the table, they continued talking, and from the general theme as to whether young folk should or should not be ambitious, they passed on to the student's hopes of some day being a millionaire.

"I'm convinced that I shall be one," said the boy. "In my family there have been a number of individuals with great luck."

"That's all very well, Roberto," muttered the old man. "But one must know how to become wealthy."

"Don't imagine that my hope is illusory; I'm going to inherit, and not a small amount, either; I'm heir to a vast sum ... millions.... The foundations of my work and the framework are already completed; all I need now is money."

Don Telmo's countenance was crossed by an expression of disagreeable surprise.

"Don't worry," replied Roberto, "I'm not going to ask you for it."

"My dear boy, if I had it, I'd give it to you with pleasure, and free of interest. They think I'm a millionaire."

"No. I tell you I'm not trying to get a cntimo from you. All I ask is a bit of advice."

"Speak, then, speak. I'm all attention," answered the old man, resting an elbow upon the table.

Manuel, who was taking off the tablecloth, cocked his ears.

At that juncture one of the salesmen entered the dining-room, and Roberto, who was about to say something, grew silent and looked impertinently at the intruder. The student was an aristocratic type with blond hair, thick and combed back, and moustache of glittering white, like silver; his skin was somewhat tanned by the sun.

"Won't you continue?" asked Don Telmo.

"No," answered the student, staring at the salesman. "For I don't want anybody to hear what I have to say."

"Come to my room, then," replied Don Telmo. "There we can talk undisturbed. We'll have coffee up in my room. Manuel!" he ordered. "Bring us two coffees."

Manuel, who was deeply interested in discovering what the student had to say, dashed out into the street on his errand. He was more than a quarter of an hour in returning with the coffee, and supposed that Roberto by this time had finished his story.

He knocked at Don Telmo's door and was resolved to linger there as long as possible, that he might catch all he could of the conversation. He began to dust Don Telmo's lamp-table with a cloth.

"And how did you ascertain that," Don Telmo was asking, "if your family didn't know it?"

"Quite by accident," answered the student. "A couple of years ago, about this time of the year, I wished to give a present to a sister, who is a protege of mine, and who

32

is very fond of playing the piano. It occurred to me, three days before her birthday, to purchase two operas, have them bound and send them to her. I wanted to have the book bound immediately, but at the shops they told me there was no time; I was walking along with my operas under my arm in the vicinity of the Plaza de las Descalzas when in the back wall of a convent I caught sight of a tiny bookbinder's shop,—like a cave with steps leading down. I asked the man,—a gnarled old fellow,—whether he would bind the book for me in a couple of days, and he said 'Yes.' 'Very well,' I told him, 'then I'll call within two days.'—'I'll send it to you; let me have your address.' I gave him my address and he asked my name. 'Roberto Hasting y Nez de Letona.'—'Are you a Nez de Latona?' he inquired, gazing at me curiously. 'Yes, sir.'— 'Do you come from la Rioja?'—'Yes, and suppose I do?' I retorted, provoked by all this questioning. And the binder, whose mother was a Nez de Latona and came from la Rioja, told me the story I've just told you. At first I took it all as a joke; then, after some time, I wrote to my mother, and she wrote back that everything was quite so, and that she recalled something of the whole matter."

Don Telmo's gaze strayed over toward Manuel.

"What are you doing here?" he snarled. "Get out; I don't want you going around telling tales...."

"I'm no tattle-tale."

"Very well, then, get a move on."

Manuel went out, and Don Telmo and Roberto continued their conversation. The boarders showered Manuel with questions, but he refused to open his mouth. He had decided to join the group of the Sensible ones.

This friendship between the old man and the student served as an incitement for the continuation of the espionage. One of the salesmen learned that Don Telmo drew up contracts of sales on reversion and made a living by lending money on houses and furniture, and at other such usurious business.

Some one saw him in the Rastro in an old clothes shop that probably belonged to him, and invented the tale that he had gold coins concealed in his room and that he played with them at night upon the bed.

It was also discovered that Don Telmo frequently paid visits to a very elegant, good looking young lady, who was, according to some, his sweetheart, and to others, his niece.

On the following Sunday Manuel overheard a conversation between the old man and the student. In a dark room there was a transom that opened into Don Telmo's room, and from this position he played the eavesdropper.

"So he refuses to furnish any more data?" Don Telmo was asking.

"Absolutely," said the student. "And he assures me that the reason for the name of Fermn de Nez de Latona not appearing in the parish register was—forgery; that this was effected by a certain Shaphter, one of Bandon's agents, and that afterwards the curates took advantage of it to acquire possession of some chaplaincies. I am certain that the town where Fermn Nez was born was either Arnedo or Autol."

Don Telmo carefully inspected a large folio document: the genealogy of Roberto's family.

"What course do you think I ought to pursue?" asked the student.

"You need money; but it's so hard to find that!" muttered the old man. "Why don't you marry?"

"And what good would that do?"

"I mean some wealthy woman...."

Here Don Telmo lowered his voice to an inaudible pitch and after a few words they separated.

The espionage of the boarders became so obstructive to the men spied upon that the Biscayan and Don Telmo served notice on the landlady of their removal. Doa Casiana's desolation, when she learned of their decision, was exceedingly great; several times she had to resort to the closet and surrender herself to the consolations of the beverage of her own concoction.

The boarders were so disappointed at the flight of the Biscayan and of Don Telmo that neither the altercations between Irene and Celia nor the stories told by the priest Don Jacinto, who stressed the smutty note, were potent enough to draw them from their silence.

The bookkeeper, a jaundiced fellow with an emaciated face and a beard like that of a monumental Jew, exceedingly taciturn and timid, had burst into speech in his excitement over the intrigues invented and fancied in the life of Don Telmo; now he became from moment to moment sallower than ever with his hypochondria.

Don Telmo's departure was paid for by the student and Don Manuel. As far as the student was concerned they dared no more than twit him on his complicity with the old man and the Biscayan; at Manuel, however, they all kept screeching and scolding when they weren't kicking him.

One of the salesmen,—the fellow who was troubled with his stomach, exasperated by the boredom, the heat and his uncertain digestion, found no other distraction than insulting and berating Manuel while he served at table, whether or not there were cause.

"Go on, you cheap fool!" he would say. "You're not worth the food you eat! Clown!"

This refrain, added to others of the same tenor, began to weary Manuel. One day the salesman heaped the insults and the vilification upon him more plentifully than ever. They had sent the boy out for two coffees, and he was slow in returning; on that particular day the delay was not due to any fault of his, for he had been kept waiting a long time.

"They ought to put a pack-saddle on you, you ass!" shouted the agent as Manuel entered.

"You won't be the one to do it!" retorted the boy impudently, as he placed the cups upon the table.

"I won't? Do you want to see me?"

"Yes, I do."

The salesman got up and kicked Manuel in the shins; the poor boy saw stars. He gave a cry of pain and then, furious, seized a plate and sent it flying at the agent's head; the latter ducked and the projectile crossed the dining-room, crashed through a window pane and fell into the courtyard, where it smashed with a racket. The salesman grabbed one of the coffee-pots that was filled with coffee and milk and hurled it at Manuel with such good aim that it struck the boy in the face; the youth, blinded with rage and by the coffee and milk, rushed upon his enemy, cornered him, and took revenge for the insults and blows with an endless succession of kicks and punches.

"He's killing me! He's killing me!" shrieked the agent in feminine wails.

"Thief! Clown!" shouted Manuel, employing the street's choicest repertory of insults.

The Superman and the priest seized Manuel by the arms, leaving him at the mercy of the salesman, who, beholding the boy thus corralled, tried to wreak vengeance; but when he was ready to strike, Manuel gave him such a forceful kick in the stomach that the fellow vomited up his whole meal.

Everybody took sides against Manuel, except Roberto, who defended him. The agent retired to his room, summoned the landlady, and told her that he refused to remain another moment as long as Petra's son was in the house.

The landlady, whose chief interest was to retain her boarder, communicated her decision to her servant.

"Now see what you've done. You can't stay here any longer," said Petra to her son.

"All right. That clown will pay for these," replied the boy, nursing the welts on his forehead. "I tell you, if I ever meet him I'm going to smash in his head."

"You take good care not to say a word to him."

At this moment the student happened to enter the dining-room.

"You did well, Manuel," he exclaimed, turning to Petra. "What right had that blockhead to insult him? In this place every boss has a right to attack his neighbour if he doesn't do as all the others wish. What a cowardly gang!"

As he spoke, Roberto blanched with rage; then he grew calm and asked Petra:

"Where are you going to take Manuel now?"

"To a cobbler's shop that belongs to a relative of mine on Aguila street."

"Is it in the poorer quarters?"

"Yes."

"I'll come to see you some day."

Before Manuel had gone to bed, Roberto appeared again in the dining-room.

"Listen," he said to Manuel. "If you know any strange place in the slums where criminals get together, let me hear. I'll go with you."

"I'll let you know, never you mind."

"Fine. See you again. Good-bye!"

Roberto extended his hand to Manuel, who pressed it with deep gratitude.

PART TWO

CHAPTER I

The Regeneration of Footwear and The Lion of The Shoemaker's
Art—The First Sunday—An Escapade—El Bizco and his Gang.

The inhabitant of Madrid who at times finds himself by accident in the poor quarters
near the Manzanares river, is surprised at the spectacle of poverty and sordidness, of
sadness and neglect presented by the environs of Madrid with their wretched Rondas,
laden with dust in the summer and in winter wallowing in mire. The capital is a city
of contrasts; it presents brilliant light in close proximity to deep gloom; refined life,
almost European, in the centre; in the suburbs, African existence, like that of an Arab
village. Some years ago, not many, in the vicinity of the Ronda de Sevilla and of el
Campillo de Gil Imn, there stood a house of suspicious aspect and of not very
favourable repute, to judge by popular rumour. The observer ...

In this and other paragraphs of the same style I had placed some hope, for they
imparted to my novel a certain phantasmagoric and mysterious atmosphere; but my
friends have convinced me I ought to suppress these passages, arguing that they
would be quite in place in a Parisian novel, but not in one dealing with Madrid,—not
at all. They add, moreover, that here nobody goes astray, not even if one wishes to.
Neither are there here any observers, nor houses of suspicious aspect, nor anything
else. In resignation, then, I have excised these paragraphs, through which I hoped
some day to be elected to the Spanish Academy; and so I continue my tale in more
pedestrian language.

It came about, then, that on the day following the row in the dining-room of the
lodging-house, Petra, very early in the morning, woke Manuel and told him to dress.

The boy recalled the scene of the previous day; he verified it by raising his hand to
his forehead, for the bruises still pained him, and from his mother's tone he
understood that she persisted in her resolve to take him to the cobbler's.

After Manuel had dressed, mother and son left the house and went into the bun-shop
for a cup of coffee and milk. Then they walked down to Arenal Street, crossed the
Plaza del Oriente, and the Viaduct, thence through Rosario Street. Continuing along
the walls of a barracks they reached the heights at whose base runs the Ronda de
Segovia. From this eminence there was a view of the yellowish countryside that
reached as far as Jetafe and Villaverde, and the San Isidro cemeteries with their grey
mudwalls and their black cypresses.

From the Ronda de Segovia, which they covered in a short time, they climbed up
Aguila Street, and paused before a house at the corner of the Campillo de Gil Imn.

There were two shoe shops opposite one another and both closed. Manuel's mother,
who could not recall which was her relative's place, inquired at the tavern.

38

"Seor Ignacio's over at the big house," answered the tavern-keeper. "I think the cobbler's come already, but he hasn't opened the shop yet."

Mother and son had to wait until the shop was opened. The building was not the tiny, evil-boding one, but it looked as if it had an atrocious desire to cave in, for here and there it, too, showed cracks, holes and all manner of disfigurements. It had a lower and upper floor, large and wide balconies the balustrades of which were gnawed by rust and the diminutive panes of glass held in place by leaden strips.

On the ground floor of the house, in the part that faced Aguila Street, there was a livery-stable, a carpenter's shop, a tavern and the cobbler's shop owned by Petra's relation. This establishment displayed over the entrance a sign that read:

For The Regeneration of Footwear.

The historian of the future will surely find in this sign proof of how widespread, during several epochs, was a certain notion of national regeneration, and it will not surprise him that this idea, which was launched in the aim to reform and regenerate the Constitution and the Spanish people, came to an end upon the signboard of a shop on a foresaken corner of the slums, where the only thing done was the reformation and regeneration of footwear.

We will not deny the influence of this regenerating theory upon the proprietor of the establishment *For The Regeneration of Footwear;* but we must point out that this presumptuous legend was put up in token of his defiance of the cobbler across the way, and we must register likewise that it had been answered by another, and even more presumptuous, one.

One fine morning the workmen in the establishment for *The Regeneration of Footwear* were dumfounded to find staring them in the face the sign of the rival shop. It was a beautiful signboard about two metres long, bearing this inscription:

The Lion of the Shoemaker's Art

This in itself was quite tolerable; the terrible, annihilating thing about it was the painting that sprawled over the middle of the board. A handsome yellow lion with the face of a man and with wavy mane, standing erect; in his front paws he held a boot, apparently of patent-leather. Beneath this representation was printed the following: *You may break, but never unstitch it.*

This was a crushing motto: A lion (wild beast) trying to unseam the boot made by the Lion (shoemaker), and powerless before the task! What a humiliation for the lion! What a triumph for the shoemaker! The lion, in this case, was *For The Regeneration of Footwear,* which, as the saying goes, had been compelled to bite the dust.

In addition to Seor Ignacio's sign there was, in one of the balconies of the large house, the bust of a woman, made probably of pasteboard, with lettering beneath: *Perfecta Ruiz: Ladies' Hair Dressing;* on the side walls of the main entrance there hung several announcements unworthy of occupying the attention of the aforementioned historian, in which were offered low-priced rooms with or without bed, amanuenses and seamstresses. A single card, upon which were pasted horizontally, vertically and obliquely a number of cut-out figures, deserved to go down in history for its laconicism. It read:

Parisian Styles. Escorihuela, Tailor.

Manuel, who had not taken the trouble to read all these signs, went into the building by a little door at the side of the livery-stable entrance, and walked through the corridor to a very filthy courtyard.

When he returned to the street the cobbler's shop had already been opened. Petra and her boy entered.

"Isn't Seor Ignacio in?" she asked.

"He'll be here in a second," answered a youngster who was piling up old shoes in the middle of the shop.

"Tell him that his cousin is here,—Petra."

Seor Ignacio appeared. He was a man of between forty and fifty, thin and wizened. Petra and he got into conversation, while the boy and a little urchin continued to heap up the old shoes. Manuel was looking on, when the boy said to him:

"Come on, you. Lend a hand!"

Manuel pitched in, and when the three had ended their labours, they waited for Petra and Seor Ignacio to finish chatting. Petra was recounting Manuel's latest exploits to her cousin and the cobbler listened smilingly. The man bore no signs of gruffness; he was blond and beardless; upon his upper lip sprouted a few saffron-hued hairs. His complexion was leathery, wrinkled; the deep furrows of his face, and his wearied mien, gave him the appearance of a weakling. He spoke with a certain ironic vagueness.

"You're going to stay here," said Petra to Manuel.

"All right."

"He's an amiable rogue," exclaimed Seor Ignacio, laughing. "He agrees right away."

40

"Yes; he takes everything calmly. But, look—" she added, turning to her son, "if ever I find out that you carry on as you did yesterday, you'll hear from me!"

Manuel said good-bye to his mother.

"Were you very long in that town of Soria with my cousin?" Seor Ignacio asked.

"Two years."

"And did you work very hard there?"

"I didn't work at all."

"Well, sonny, you can't get out of it here. Come. Sit down and get busy. These are your cousins," added Seor Ignacio, indicating the youth and the little boy.

"They are a pair of warriors, too."

The youth's name was Leandro, and he was well-built; in no respect did he resemble his father. He had thick lips and a thick nose, an obstinate, manly expression; the other was a boy of about Manuel's age, frail, thin, with a rascally look, and called Vidal.

Seor Ignacio and the three boys sat down around a wooden block formed of a tree-trunk with a deep groove running through it. The labour consisted in undoing and taking apart old boots and shoes, which arrived at the shop from every direction in huge, badly tied bales and in sacks with paper designations sewed to the burlap. The boot destined to be drawn and quartered was laid upon the block; there it received a stroke or more from a knife until the heel was severed; then, with the nippers the various layers of sole were ripped off; with the scissors they cut off buttons and laces, and everything was sorted into its corresponding basket: in one, the heels; in others, the rubbers, the latchets, the buckles.

So low had *The Regeneration of Footwear* descended: it justified its title in a manner quite distinct from that intended by the one who had bestowed it.

Seor Ignacio, a master workman, had been compelled through lack of business to abandon the awl and the shoemaker's stirrup for the nippers and the knife; creating for destroying; the fashioning of new boots for the disembowelling of old. The contrast was bitter; but Seor Ignacio could find consolation in looking across at his neighbour, he of the *Lion of The Shoemaker's Art*, who only at rare intervals would receive an order for some cheap pair of boots.

The first morning of work was infinitely boresome to Manuel; this protracted inactivity became unbearable. At noon a bulky old woman entered the shop with their lunch in a basket. This was Seor Ignacio's mother.

"And my wife?" the cobbler asked her.

"She's gone washing."

"And Salom Isn't she coming?"

"No. She got some work in a house for the whole week."

The old lady extracted from the basket a pot, dishes, napkins, cutlery, and a huge loaf of bread; she laid a cloth upon the floor and everybody squatted down around it. She poured the soup from the pot into the plates, into which each one crumbled a bit of bread, and they began to eat. Then the old woman doled out to each his portion of boiled meat and vegetables, and, as they ate, the cobbler discoursed briefly upon the future of Spain and the reasons for national backwardness,—a topic that appeals to most Spaniards, who consider themselves regenerators.

Seor Ignacio was a mild liberal, a man who swelled with enthusiasm over these words about the national sovereignty, and who spoke openly of the Glorious Revolution. In matters of religion he advocated freedom of worship; his ideal would be for Spain to have an equal number of priests of the Catholic, Protestant, Jewish and every other denomination, for thus, he asserted, each would choose the dogma that seemed to him best. But one thing he'd certainly do if he had a say in the government. He would expel all the monks and nuns, for they're like the mange: the weaker the sufferer, the more it thrives. To this argument Leandro, the elder son, added that as far as the monks, nuns and other small fry were concerned, the best course with them was to lop off their heads like hogs, and with regard to the priests, whether Catholic, Protestant or Chinese, nothing would be lost if there were nary a one.

The old lady, too, joined the conversation, and since to her, as a huckstress of vegetables, politics was chiefly a question between marketwomen and the municipal guards, she spoke of a row in which the amiable ladies of the Cebada market had discharged their garden produce at the heads of several redcoats who were defending a trouble-maker of the market. The huckstresses wanted to organize a union, and then lay down the law and fix prices. Now this didn't at all appeal to her.

"What the deuce!" she exclaimed. "What right have they to take away a person's stock if he wants to sell it cheaper? Suppose I take it into my head to give it all away free."

"Why no, seora," differed Leandro. "That's not right."

"And why not?"

"Because it isn't. Because tradesfolk ought to help one another, and if you, let's suppose, do as you say, you prevent somebody else from selling, and that's why Socialism was invented,—to favour man's industry."

"All right, then. Let them give two duros to man's industry and kill it."

The woman spoke very phlegmatically and sententiously. Her calm manner harmonized perfectly with her huge person, which was as thick and rigid as a tree-trunk; her face was fleshy and of stolid features, her wrinkles deep; pouches of loose flesh sagged beneath her eyes; on her head she wore a black kerchief, tightly knotted around her temples.

Seora Jacoba—that was her name—was a woman who probably felt neither heat nor cold; summer and winter she spent the dead hours seated by her vegetable stand at the Puerta de Moros; if she sold a head of lettuce between sunrise and sunset, it was a great deal.

After eating, some of the shoemaker's family went off to the courtyard for their siesta, while others remained in the shop.

Vidal, the man's younger son, sprawled out in the patio beside Manuel, and having inquired into the cause of the bumps that stood out on his cousin's forehead, asked:

"Have you ever been on this street before?"

"I? No."

"We have great times around here."

"You do, eh?"

"I should say so. Haven't you a girl?"

"I? No."

"Well, there are lots of girls 'round here that would like to have a fellow."

"Really?"

"Yes, sir! Over where we live there's a very pretty little thing, a friend of my girl. You can hitch up with her."

"But don't you live in this house?"

43

"No. We live in Embajadores lane. It's my aunt Salom and my grandmother who live here. Over where we are—oh, boy!—the times I've had!"

"In the town where I come from," said Manuel, not to be dwarfed by his cousin, "there were mountains higher than twenty of your houses here."

"In Madrid we've got the Monte de Prncipe Pio."

"But it can't be as high as the one in that town."

"It can't? Why, in Madrid everything's the best."

Manuel was not a little put out by the superiority which his cousin tried to assume by speaking to him about women in the tone of an experienced man about town who knew them through and through. After the noonday nap and a game of mus, over which the shoemaker and a few neighbours managed to get into a wrangle, Seor Ignacio and his children went off to their house. Manuel supped at Seora Jacoba's, the vegetable huckstress's, and slept in a beautiful bed that looked to him far better than the one at the boarding-house.

Once in, he weighed the pros and contras of his new social position, and in the midst of his calculations as to whether the needle of the balance inclined to this side or that, he fell asleep.

At first, the monotony of the labour and the steady application bothered Manuel; but soon he grew accustomed to one thing and another, so that the days seemed shorter and the work less irksome.

The first Sunday Manuel was fast asleep in Seora Jacoba's house when Vidal came in and waked him. It was after eleven; the marketwoman, as usual, had departed at dawn for her stall, leaving the boy alone.

"What are you doing there?" asked Vidal. "Why don't you get up?"

"Why? What time is it?"

"Awful late."

Manuel dressed hurriedly and they both left the house. Nearby, opposite Aguila street, on a little square, they joined a group of boys who were playing *chito*, and they followed the fortunes of the game with deep interest.

At noon Vidal said to his cousin:

"Today we're going to eat yonder."

"At your house?"

"Yes. Come on."

Vidal, whose specialty was finding things, discovered close by the fountain of the Ronda, which is near Aguila Street, an old, wide-brimmed high hat; the poor thing was hidden in a corner, perhaps through modesty. He began to kick it along and send it flying through the air and Manuel joined in the enterprise, so that between the two they transported the relic, venerable with antiquity, from the Ronda de Segovia to that of Toledo, thence to the Ronda de Embajadores, until they abandoned it in the middle of the street, minus top and brim. Having committed this perversity, Manuel and Vidal debouched into the Paseo da las Acacias and went into a house whose entrance consisted of a doorless archway.

The two boys walked through a narrow passage paved with cobblestones until they reached a courtyard, and then, by one of the numerous staircases they climbed to the balcony of the first floor, on which opened a row of doors and windows all painted blue.

"Here's where we live," said Vidal, pointing to one of the doors.

They entered. Seor Ignacio's home was small; it comprised two bedrooms, a parlour, the kitchen and a dark room. The first habitation was the parlour, furnished with a pine bureau, a sofa, several straw chairs and a green mirror stuck with chromos and photographs and covered with red netting. The cobbler's family used the parlour as the dining-room on Sundays, because it was the lightest and the most spacious of their rooms.

When Manuel and Vidal arrived the family had been waiting for them a long time. They all sat down to table, and Salom, the cobbler's sister-in-law, took charge of serving the meal. She resembled very closely her sister, the mother of Vidal. Both, of medium height, had short, saucy noses and black, pretty eyes; despite this physical similarity, however, their appearance differentiated them sharply. Vidal's mother,— called Leandra,—untidy, unkempt, loathsome, and betraying traces of ill humour, seemed much older than Salom, although but three or four years separated them. Salom had a merry, resolute air.

Yet, consider the irony of fate! Leandra, despite her slovenly ways, her sour disposition and her addiction to drink, was married to a good hardworking man, while Salom, endowed with excellent gifts of industriousness and sweet temper, had wound up by going to live with an outcast who made his way by swindling, pilfering and browbeating and who had given her two children. Her humble or servile spirit, confronted with this wild, independent nature, made Salom adore her man, and she deceived herself into considering him a tremendous, energetic fellow, though he was in all truth a coward and a tramp. The bully had seen just how matters stood, and whenever it pleased him he would stamp into the house and demand the pay that Salom earned by sewing at the machine, at five cntimos per two yards. Unresistingly she handed him the product of her sweating toil, and many a time the ruffian, not content with depriving her of the money, gave her a beating into the bargain.

Salom's two children were not today in Seor Ignacio's home; on Sundays, after dressing them very neatly, their mother would send them to a relative of hers,—the proprietress of a workshop,—where they spent the afternoon.

At the meal Manuel listened to the conversation without taking part. They were discussing one of the girls of the neighbourhood who had run off with a wealthy horse-dealer, a married man with a family.

"She did wisely," declared Leandra, draining a glass of wine.

"If she didn't know he was married...."

"What's the difference?" retorted Leandra with an air of unconcern.

"Plenty. How would you like a woman to carry off your husband?" Salom asked her sister.

"Psch!"

"Yes, nowadays, we know," interrupted Seor Ignacio's mother. "Of two women there isn't one that's respectable."

"A great ways any one'll go by being respectable," snarled Leandra. "Poverty and hunger.... If a woman weren't to get married, then she might make a change and even acquire money."

"I don't see how," asserted Salom.

"How? Even if she had to go into the business."

Seor Ignacio, disgusted, turned his head away from his wife, and his elder son, Leandro, eyed his mother grimly, severely.

"Bah, that's all talk," argued Salom, who wished to thresh the matter out impersonally. "You'd hardly like it just the same if folks were to insult you wherever you went."

"Me? Much I care what folks say to me!" replied the cobbler's wife. "Stuff and nonsense! If they call me a loose woman, and if I'm not, why, you see: a floral wreath. And if I am,—it's all the same in the end."

Seor Ignacio, offended, shifted the conversation to the crime on Pauelas Street; a jealous organ-grinder had slain his sweetheart for a harsh word and the hearers were excited over the case, each offering his opinion. The meal over, Seor Ignacio, Leandro, Vidal and Manuel went out to the gallery to have a nap while the women remained inside gossiping.

All the neighbours had brought their sleeping-mats out, and in their undershirts, half naked, some seated, others stretched out, they were dozing on the galleries.

"Hey, you," said Vidal to Manuel. "Let's be off."

"Where?"

"To the Pirates. We meet today. They must be waiting for us already."

"What do you mean,—pirates?"

"Bizco and the others."

"And why do they call 'em that?"

"Because they're like the old time pirates."

Manuel and Vidal stepped into the patio and leaving the house, walked off down Embajadores lane.

"They call us the Pirates," explained Vidal, "from a certain battle of stones we had. Some of the kids from the Paseo de las Acacias had got some sticks and formed a company with a Spanish flag at the head; then I, Bizco, and three or four others, began to throw stones at them and made them retreat. The Corretor, a fellow who lives in our house, and who saw us chasing after them, said to us: 'Say, are you pirates or what? For, if you're pirates you ought to fly the black flag. Well, next day I swiped a dark apron from my father and I tied it to a stick and we got after the kids with the Spanish flag and came near making them surrender it. That's why they call us the Pirates."

The two cousins came to a tiny, squalid district.

"This is the Casa del Cabrero," said Vidal. "And here are our chums."

So it proved; the entire pirate gang was here encamped. Manuel now made the acquaintance of El Bizco, a cross-eyed species of chimpanzee, square-shaped, husky, long-armed, with misshapen legs and huge red hands.

"This is my cousin," added Vidal, introducing Manuel to the gang; and then, to make him seem interesting, he told how Manuel had come to the house with two immense lumps that he had received in a Homeric struggle with a man.

Bizco stared closely at Manuel, and seeing that Manuel, on his side, was observing him calmly, averted his gaze. Bizco's face possessed the interest of a queer animal or of a pathological specimen. His narrow forehead, his flat nose, his thick lips, his freckled skin and his red, wiry hair lent him the appearance of a huge, red baboon.

As soon as Vidal had arrived, the gang mobilized and all the ragamuffins went foraging through la Casa del Cabrero.

This was the name given to a group of low tenement hovels that bounded a long, narrow patio. At this hot hour the men and women, stretched out half naked on the ground, were sleeping in the shade as in a trance. Some women, in shifts, huddled into a circle of four or five, were smoking the same cigar, each taking a puff and passing it along from hand to hand.

A swarm of naked brats infested the place; they were the colour of the soil, most of them black, some fair, with blue eyes. As if already they felt the degradation of their poverty, these urchins neither shouted nor frolicked about the yard.

A few lasses of ten to fourteen were chatting in a group. Bizco, Vidal and the rest of the gang gave chase to them around the patio. The girls, half naked, dashed off, shrieking and shouting insults.

Bizco boasted that he had violated some of the girls.

"They're all *puchereras* like the ones on Ceres Street," said one of the Pirates.

"So they make pots, do they?" inquired Manuel.

"Yes. Fine pots, all right!"

"Then why do you call them *puchereras*?"

"Becau—" added the urchin, and he made a coarse gesture.

"Because they're a sly bunch," stammered Bizco. "You're awful simple."

Manuel contemplated Bizco scornfully, and asked his cousin:

"Do you mean to say that those little girls...?"

"They and their mothers," answered Vidal philosophically. "Almost all of 'em that live here."

The Pirates left the Casa del Cabrero, descended an embarkment after passing a high, black fence, and at the middle of Casa Blanca turned into the Paseo de Yeseras.

They approached the morgue, a white structure near the river, situated at the foot of the Dehesa del Canal. They circled around it, trying to catch a glimpse of some corpse, but the windows were closed.

They continued along the banks of the Manzanares, amidst the twisted pines of la Dehesa. The river ran very thin, consisting of a few threads of murky water and pools above the mud.

At the end of the Dehesa de la Arganzuela, opposite a large, spacious lot surrounded by a fence made of flattened oil cans nailed to posts, the gang paused to inspect the place, whose wide area was taken up with watering-carts, mechanical sweepers, ditch pumps, heaps of brooms and other tools and appurtenances of municipal cleanliness.

In one corner of the lot arose a white edifice that, judging from its two towers and the vacant belfries, had formerly been a church or a convent.

The gang went nosing about the place and passed under an arch bearing the inscription: "Stallion Stables." Behind the structure that looked like a convent they came upon some shanties furnished with filthy, grimy mats: African huts built upon a framework of rough sticks and cane.

Bizco went into one of these hovels and returned with a piece of cod in his hand.

Manuel was overcome by a horrible fear.

"I'm going," he said to Vidal.

"What do you mean!..." exclaimed one of the gang ironically. "Much nerve you've got!"

All at once another of the urchins cried:

"Skip. Somebody's coming!"

The pirates started on a run down the Paseo del Canal.

Madrid, with its yellowish dwellings veiled in a cloud of dust, came into view. The high window-panes were aglow with the reflection of the setting sun. From the

Paseo del Canal, crossing a stubble patch, they reached the Plaza de las Peuelas, then, after going up another street they climbed the Paseo de las Acacias.

They entered the Corraln. Manuel and Vidal, after having arranged to meet the gang on the following Sunday, climbed the stairway to Seor Ignacio's house and as they drew near to the cobbler's door they heard cries.

"Father's giving the old lady a beating," murmured Vidal. "There won't be much to eat today. I'm going off to sleep."

"And how do I get to the other house?" asked Manuel.

"All you have to do is walk along the Ronda until you reach the Aguila street stairway. You can't miss it."

Manuel followed the directions. It was fearfully hot; the air was thick with dust. A few men were playing cards in tavern doorways, and in others they were dancing in embrace to the strains of a barrel-organ.

When Manuel reached the Aguila Street stairway it was getting dark. He sat down to rest a while in the Campillo de Gil Imn. From this elevated point could be seen the yellowish country, growing darker and darker with approaching night, and the chimneys and housetops sharply outlined against the horizon. The sky, blue and green above, was flushed with red nearer the earth; it darkened and assumed sinister hues,—coppery reds, purplish reds.

Above the mudwalls jutted the turrets and the cypresses of San Isidro cemetery; a round cupola stood out clearly in the atmosphere; at its top rose an angel with wings outspread, as if about to take flight against the flaming, blood-red background of evening.

Above the embanked clouds of the twilight shone a pale star in a green border, and on the horizon, animated by the last breath of day, could be discerned the hazy silhouettes of distant mountains.

CHAPTER II

The "Big Yard," or Uncle Rilo's House—Local Enmities.

When Salom finished her sewing and went off to Aguila Street to sleep, Manuel definitively settled in the home of Uncle Rilo, of Embajadores lane. Some called this La Corrala, others, El Corraln, still others, La Piltra, and it boasted so many other names that it seemed as if the neighbours spent hours and hours thinking up new designations for it.

The Corraln (Big yard)—this was the best known name of Uncle Rilo's lair,—fronted the Paseo de las Acacias, but it was not in the direct line of this thoroughfare, as it set somewhat back. The faade of this tenement, low, narrow, kalso-mined, indicated neither the depth nor the size of the building; the front revealed a few ill-shaped windows and holes unevenly arranged, while a doorless archway gave access to a narrow passage paved with cobblestones; this, soon widening, formed a patio surrounded by high, gloomy walls.

From the sides of the narrow entrance passage rose brick stairways leading to open galleries that ran along the three stories of the house and returned to the patio. At intervals, in the back of these galleries, opened rows of doors painted blue with a black number on the lintel of each.

Between the lime and the bricks of the walls stuck out, like exposed bones, jamb-posts and crossbeams, surrounded by lean bass ropes. The gallery columns, as well as the lintels and the beams that supported them, must formerly have been painted green, but as the result of the constant action of sun and rain only a stray patch of the original colour remained.

The courtyard was always filthy; in one corner lay a heap of useless scraps covered by a sheet of zinc; one could make out grimy cloths, decayed planks, debris, bricks, tiles, baskets: an infernal jumble. Every afternoon some of the women would do their washing in the patio, and when they finished their work they would empty their tubs on to the ground, and the big pools, on drying, would leave white stains and indigo rills of bluing. The neighbours also had the habit of throwing their rubbish anywhere at all, and when it rained—since the mouth of the drain would always become clogged—an unbearable, pestilential odour would rise from the black, stagnant stream that inundated the patio, and on its surface floated cabbage leaves and greasy papers.

Each neighbour could leave his tools and things in the section of the gallery that bounded his dwelling; from the looks of this area one might deduce the grade of poverty or relative comfort of each family,—its predilections and its tastes.

This space usually revealed an attempt at cleanliness and a curious aspect; here the wall was whitewashed, there hung a cage,—a few flowers in earthenware pots;

elsewhere a certain utilitarian instinct found vent in the strings of garlic put out to dry or clusters of grape suspended; beyond, a carpenter's bench and a tool-chest gave evidence of the industrious fellow who worked during his free hours.

In general, however, one could see only dirty wash hung out on the balustrades, curtains made of mats, quilts mended with patches of ill-assorted colors, begrimed rags stretched over broomsticks or suspended from ropes tied from one post to the other, that they might get a trifle more light and air.

Every section of the gallery was a manifestation of a life apart within this communism of hunger; this edifice contained every grade and shade of poverty: from the heroic, garbed in clean, decent tatters, to the most nauseating and repulsive.

In the majority of the rooms and holes of La Corrala one was struck immediately by the resigned, indolent indigence combined with organic and moral impoverishment.

In the space belonging to the cobbler's family, at the tip of a very long pole attached to one of the pillars, waved a pair of patch-covered trousers comically balancing itself.

Off from the large courtyard of El Corraln branched a causeway heaped with ordure, leading to a smaller courtyard that in winter was converted into a fetid swamp.

A lantern, surrounded with a wire netting to prevent the children from breaking it with stones, hung from one of the black walls.

In the inner courtyard the rooms were much cheaper than those of the large patio; most of them brought twenty-three reales, but there were some for two or three pesetas per month: dismal dens with no ventilation at all, built in the spaces under stairways and under the roof.

In some moister climate La Corrala would have been a nest of contagion: the wind and sun of Madrid, however,—that sun which brings blisters to the skin,—saw to the disinfection of that pesthole.

As if to make sure that terror and tragedy should haunt the edifice, one saw, on entering,—either at the main door or in the corridor,—a drunken, delirious hag who begged alms and spat insults at everybody. They called her Death. She must have been very old, or at least appeared so. Her gaze was wandering, her look diffident, her face purulent with scabs; one of her lower eyelids, drawn in as the result of some ailment, exposed the bloody, turbid inside of her eyeball. Death would stalk about in her tatters, in house slippers, with a tin-box and an old basket into which she gathered her findings. Through certain superstitious considerations none dared to throw her into the street.

52

On his very first night in La Corrala Manuel verified, not without a certain astonishment, the truth of what Vidal had told him. That youngster, and almost all the gamins of his age, had sweethearts among the little girls of the tenement, and it was not a rare occurrence, as he passed by some nook, to come upon a couple that jumped up and ran away.

The little children amused themselves playing bull-fight, and among the most-applauded feats was that of Don Tancredo. One tot would get down on all fours, and another, not very heavy, would mount him and fold his arms, thrust back his chest and place a three-cornered hat of paper upon his erect, haughty head.

He who was playing the bull would approach, roar loudly, sniff Don Tancredo and pass by without throwing him over; a couple of times he would repeat this, and then dash off. Whereupon Don Tancredo would dismount from his living pedestal to receive the plaudits of the public. There were wily, waggish bulls who took it into their heads to pull both statue and pedestal to the ground, and this would be received amidst shouts and huzzahs of the spectators.

In the meantime the girls would be playing in a ring, the women would shout from gallery to gallery and the men would chat in their shirtsleeves; some fellow, squatting on the floor, would scrape away monotonously at the strings of a guitar.

La Muerte, the old beggar, would also cheer the evening gatherings with her long discourse.

La Corrala was a seething, feverish world in little, as busy as an anthill. There people toiled, idled, guzzled, ate and died of hunger; there furniture was made, antiques were counterfeited, old embroideries were fashioned, buns cooked, broken porcelain mended, robberies planned and women's favours traded.

La Corrala was a microcosm; it was said that if all the denizens were placed in line they would reach from Embajadores lane to the Plaza del Progreso; it harboured men who were everything and yet nothing: half scholars, half smiths, half carpenters, half masons, half business men, half thieves.

In general, everybody who lived here was disoriented, dwelling in that unending abjection produced by everlasting, irremediable poverty; many sloughed their occupations as a reptile its skin; others had none; some carpenters' or masons' helpers, because of their lack of initiative, understanding and skill, could never graduate from their apprenticeship. There were also gypsies, mule and dog clippers, nor was there a dearth of porters, itinerant barbers and mountebanks. Almost all of them, if opportunity offered, stole what they could; they all presented the same pauperized, emaciated look. And all harboured a constant rage that vented itself in furious imprecations and blasphemies.

They lived as if sunk in the shades of a deep slumber, unable to form any clear notion of their lives, without aspirations, aims, projects or anything.

There were some whom a couple of glasses of wine made drunk for half a week; others seemed already besotted, without having had a sip, and their countenances constantly mirrored the most absolute debasement, whence they escaped only in a fleeting moment of anger or indignation.

Money was to them, more often than not, a misfortune. Possessing an instinctive understanding of their weakness and their frail wills, they would resort to the tavern in quest of courage; there they would cast off all restraint, shout, argue, forget the sorrows of the moment, feel generous, and when, after having bragged to the top of their bent they believed themselves ready for anything, they discovered that they hadn't a cntimo and that the illusory strength imbibed with the alcohol was evaporating.

The women of the house, as a rule, worked harder than the men, and were almost always disputing. For thirty years past they had all shared the same character and represented almost the same type: foul, unkempt, termagacious, they—shrieked and grew desperate upon the slightest provocation.

From time to time, like a gentle sunbeam amidst the gloom, the souls of these stultified, bestial men,—of these women embittered by harsh lives that held neither solace nor illusion,—would be penetrated by a romantic, disinterested feeling of tenderness that made them live like human beings for a while; but when the gust of sentimentalism had blown over, they would return to their moral inertia, as resigned and passive as ever. The permanent neighbours of La Corrala were situated in the floors surrounding the large courtyard. In the other courtyard the majority were transients, and spent, at most, a couple of weeks in the house. Then, as the saying was among them, they spread wing.

One day a mender would appear with his huge bag, his brace and his pliers, shouting through the streets in a husky voice: "Jars and tubs to mend ... pans, dishes and plates!" After a short stay he would be off; the following week arrived a dealer in cloth bargains, crying at the top of his lungs his silk handkerchiefs at ten and fifteen cntimos; another day came an itinerant hawker, his cases laden with pins, combs and brooches, or some purchaser of gold and silver braid. Certain seasons of the year brought a contingent of special types; spring announced itself through the appearance of mule dealers, tinkers, gypsies and bohemians; in autumn swarmed bands of rustics with cheese from La Mancha and pots of honey, while winter brought the walnut and chestnut vendors.

Of the permanent tenants in the first courtyard, those who were intimate with Seor Ignacio included: a proof-corrector, nick-named El Corretor; a certain Rebolledo, both barber and inventor, and four blind men, who were known by the sobriquets El Calabazas, El Sapistas, El Erigido and El Cuco and dwelt in harmony with their respective wives playing the latest tangos, *tientos* and *zarzuela* ditties on the streets.

54

The proof-reader had a numerous family: his wife, his mother-in-law, a daughter of twenty and a litter of tots; the pay he earned correcting proof at a newspaper office was not enough for his needs and he used to suffer dire straits. He was in the habit of wearing a threadbare macfarland,—frayed at the edges,—a large, dirty handkerchief tied around his throat, and a soft, yellow, grimy slouch hat.

His daughter, Milagros by name, a slender lass as sleek as a bird, had relations with Leandro, Manual's cousin.

The sweethearts had plenty of love quarrels, now because of her flirtations, now because of the evil life he led.

They could not get along, for Milagros was a bit haughty and a climber, considering herself a social superior fallen upon evil days, while Leandro, on the other hand, was abrupt and irascible.

The cobbler's other neighbour, Seor Zurro, a quaint, picturesque type, had nothing to do with Seor Ignacio and felt for the proof-reader a most cordial hatred. El Zurro went about forever concealed behind a pair of blue spectacles, wearing a fur cap and ample cassock.

"His name is Zurro (fox)," the proof-reader would say, "but he's a fox in his actions as well; one of those country foxes that are masters of malice and trickery."

According to popular rumour, El Zurro knew what he was about; he had a place at the lower end of the Rastro, a dark, pestilent hovel cluttered with odds and ends, second-hand coats, remnants of old cloth, tapestries, parts of chasubles, and in addition, empty bottles, flasks full of brandy and cognac, seltzer water siphons, shattered clocks, rusty muskets, keys, pistols, buttons, medals and other frippery.

Despite the fact that surely no more than a couple of persons entered Seor Zurro's shop throughout the livelong day and spent no more than a couple of reales, the second-hand dealer thrived.

He lived with his daughter Encarna, a coarse specimen of some twenty-five years, exceedingly vulgar and the personification of insolence, who went walking with her father on Sundays, bedecked with jewelry. Encarna's bosom was consumed with the fires of passion for Leandro; but that ingrate, enamoured of Milagros, was unscathed by the soul-flames of the second-hand dealer's daughter.

Wherefore Encarna mortally hated Milagros and the members of her family; every hour of the day she branded them as vulgarians, starvelings, and insulted them with such scoffing sobriquets as Mendrugo, "Beggar's Crumb," which was applied by her to the proof-reader, and "The Madwoman of the Vatican," which meant his daughter.

It was not at all rare for such hatreds, between persons forced almost into living in common, to grow to violent rancour and malevolence; thus, the members of one and the other family never looked at each other without exchanging curses and wishes for the most disastrous misfortunes.

CHAPTER III

Roberto Hastings at the Shoemaker's—Procession of Beggars—Court of Miracles.

One morning toward the end of September Roberto appeared in the doorway of *The Regeneration of Footwear*, and thrusting his head into the shop exclaimed:

"Hello, Manuel!"

"Hello, Don Roberto!"

"Working, eh?"

Manuel shrugged his shoulders, indicating that the job was not exactly to his taste.

Roberto hesitated for a moment, but at last made up his mind and entered the shop.

"Have a seat," invited Seor Ignacio, offering him a chair.

"Are you Manuel's uncle?"

"At your service."

Roberto sat down, offered a cigar to Seor Ignacio and another to Leandro, and the three began to smoke.

"I know your nephew," said Roberto to the proprietor, "for I live in the house where Petra works."

"You do?"

"And I wish you'd let him off today for a couple of hours."

"All right, seor. All afternoon, if you wish."

"Fine. Then I'll call for him after lunch."

"Very well."

Roberto watched them work for a while, then suddenly jumped up and left.

57

Manuel could not understand what Roberto wanted, and in the afternoon waited for him with genuine impatience. Roberto carne, and the pair turned out of Aguila Street down toward the Ronda de Segovia.

"Do you know where La Doctrina is?" Roberto asked Manuel.

"What Doctrina?"

"A place where herds of beggars meet every Friday."

"I don't know."

"Do you know where the San Isidro highway is?"

"Yes."

"Good. For that's where we're going. That's where La Doctrina is."

Manuel and Roberto walked down the Paseo de los Pontones and continued in the direction of Toledo Bridge. The student was silent and Manuel did not care to ask any questions.

It was a dry, dusty day. The stifling south wind whirled puffs of heat and sand; a stray bolt of lightning illuminated the clouds; from the distance came the rumble of thunder; the landscape lay yellow under a blanket of dust.

Over the Toledo Bridge trudged a procession of beggars, both men and women, each dirtier and more tattered than the next. Out of las Cambroneras and las Injurias streamed recruits for this ragged army; they came, too, from the Paseo Imperial and from Ocho Hilos, and by this time forming solid ranks, they trooped on to the Toledo Bridge and tramped up the San Isidro highway until they reached a red edifice, before which they came to a halt.

"This must be La Doctrina," said Roberto to Manuel, pointing to a building that had a patio with a statue of Christ in the centre.

The two friends drew near to the gate. This was a beggars' conclave, a Court of Miracles assembly. The women took up almost the entire courtyard; at one end, near a chapel, the men were huddled together; one could see nothing but swollen, stupid faces, inflamed nostrils, and twisted mouths; old women as fat and clumsy as melancholy whales; little wizened, cadaverous hags with sunken mouths and noses like the beak of a bird of prey; shamefaced female mendicants, their wrinkled chins bristling with hair, their gaze half ironical and half shy; young women, thin and emaciated, slatternly and filthy; and all, young and old alike, clad in threadbare garments that had been mended, patched and turned inside out until there wasn't a

58

square inch that had been left untouched. The green, olive-coloured cloaks and the drab city garb jostled against the red and yellow short skirts of the countrywomen.

Roberto sauntered about, peering eagerly info the courtyard. Manuel trailed after him indifferently.

A large number of the beggars was blind; there were cripples, minus hand or foot, some hieratic, taciturn, solemn, others restless. Brown long-sleeved loose coats mingled with frayed sack-coats and begrimed smocks. Some of the men in tatters carried, slung over their shoulders, black sacks and game-bags; others huge cudgels in their hands; one burly negro, his face tattooed with deep stripes,— doubtless a slave in former days,—leaned against the wall in dignified indifference, clothed in rags; barefoot urchins and mangy dogs scampered about amongst the men and women; the swarming, agitated, palpitating throng of beggars seethed like an anthill.

"Let's go," said Roberto. "Neither of the women I'm looking for is here.... Did you notice," he added, "how few human faces there are among men! All you can read in the features of these wretches is mistrust, abjection, malice, just as among the rich you find only solemnity, gravity, pedantry. It's curious, isn't it? All cats have the face of cats; all oxen look like oxen; while the majority of human beings haven't a human semblance."

Roberto and Manuel left the patio. They sat down opposite La Doctrina, on the other side of the road, amid some sandy clearings.

"These doings of mine," began Roberto, "may strike you as queer. But they won't seem so strange when I tell you that I'm looking for two women here; one of them a poor beggar who can make me rich; the other, a rich lady, who perhaps would make me poor."

Manuel stared at Roberto in amazement. He had always harboured a certain suspicion that there was something wrong with the student's head.

"No. Don't imagine this is silly talk. I'm on the trail of a fortune,—a huge fortune. If you help me, I'll remember you."

"Sure. What do you want me to do?"

"I'll tell you when the right moment comes."

Manuel could not conceal an ironic smile.

"You don't believe it," muttered Roberto.

"That doesn't matter. When you'll see, you'll believe."

"Naturally."

"If I should happen to need you, promise you'll help me."

"I'll help you as far as I am able," replied Manuel, with feigned earnestness.

Several ragamuffins sprawled themselves out on the clearing near Manuel and Roberto, and the student did not care to go on with his tale.

"They've already begun to split up into divisions," said one of the loafers who wore a coachman's hat, pointing with a stick to the women inside the courtyard of La Doctrina.

And so it was; groups were clustering about the trees of the patio, on each of which was hung a poster with a picture and a number in the middle.

"There go the marchionesses," added he of the coachman's hat, indicating several women garbed in black who had just appeared in the courtyard.

The white faces stood out amidst the mourning clothes.

"They're all marchionesses," said one.

"Well, they're not all beauties," retorted Manuel, joining the conversation. "What have they come here for?"

"They're the ones who teach religion," answered the fellow with the hat. "From time to time they hand out sheets and underwear to the women and the men. Now they're going to call the roll."

A bell began to clang; the gate closed; groups were formed, and a lady entered the midst of each.

"Do you see that one there?" asked Roberto. "She's Don Telmo's niece."

"That blonde?"

"Yes. Wait for me here."

Roberto walked down the road toward the gate.

The reading of the religious lesson began; from the patio came the slow, monotonous drone of prayer.

Manuel lay back on the ground. Yonder, flat beneath the grey horizon, loomed Madrid out of the mist of the dust-laden atmosphere. The wide bed of the Manzanares river, ochre-hued, seemed furrowed here and there by a thread of dark water. The ridges of the Guadarrama range rose hazily into the murky air.

Roberto passed by the patio. The humming of the praying mendicants continued. An old lady, her head swathed in a red kerchief and her shoulders covered with a black cloak that was fading to green, sat down in the clearing.

"What's the matter, old lady? Wouldn't they open the gate for you?" shouted the fellow with the coachman's hat.

"No.... The foul old witches!"

"Don't you care. They're not giving away anything today. The distribution takes place this coming Friday. They'll give you at least a sheet," added he of the hat mischievously.

"If they don't give me anything more than a sheet," shrilled the hag, twisting her blobber-lip, "I'll tell them to keep it for themselves. The foxy creatures! ..."

"Oh, they've found you out, granny!" exclaimed one of the loafers lying on the ground. "You're a greedy one, you are."

The bystanders applauded these words, which came from a *zarzuela*, and the chap in the coachman's hat continued explaining to Manuel the workings of La Doctrina.

"There are some men and women who enrol in two and even three divisions so as to get all the charity they can," he went on. "Why, we—my father and I—once enrolled in four divisions under four different names.... And what a rumpus was raised! What a row we had with the marchionesses!"

"And what did you want with all those sheets," Manuel asked him.

"Why! Sell 'em, of course. They re sold here at the very gate at two *chuls* apiece."

"I'm going to buy one," said a coachman from a nearby hackstand, approaching the group. "I'll give it a coating of linseed oil, then varnish it and make me a cowled waterproof."

"But the marchionesses,—don't they see that these people sell their gifts right away?"

"Much they see!"

To these idlers the whole business was nothing more than a pious recreation of the religious ladies, of whom they spoke with patronizing irony.

The reading of the religious lesson did not last quite an hour.

A bell rang; the gate was swung open; the various groups dissolved and merged; everybody arose and the women began to walk off, balancing their chairs upon their heads, shouting, shoving one another violently; two or three huckstresses peddled their wares as the tattered crowd issued through the gate in a jam, shrieking as if in escape from some imminent danger. A few old women ran clumsily down the road; others huddled into a corner to urinate, and all of them were howling at the top of their lungs, overcome by the necessity of insulting the women of La Doctrina, as if instinctively they divined the uselessness of a sham charity that remedied nothing. One heard only protests and manifestation of scorn.

"Damn it all! These women of God...."

"And they want a body to have faith in 'em."

"The old drunkards."

"Let them have faith, and the mother that bore 'em."

"Let 'em give blood-pudding to everybody."

After the women came the men,—blind, maimed, crippled,—in leisurely fashion, and conversing solemnly.

"Huh! They don't want me to marry!" grumbled a blind fellow, sarcastically, turning to a cripple.

"And what do you say," asked the latter.

"I? What the deuce! Let them get married if they have any one to marry 'em. They came here and bore us stiff with their prayers and sermons. What we need isn't sermons, but hard cash and plenty of it."

"That's what, man ... the dough,—that's what we want."

"And all the rest is nothing but ... chatter and chin music.... Anybody can give advice. When it comes to bread, though, not a sign of it."

"So say I!"

The ladies came out, prayer-books in hand; the old beggar-women set off in pursuit and harassed them with entreaties.

Manuel looked everywhere for the student; at last he caught sight of him with Don Telmo's niece. The blonde turned around to look at him, and then stepped into a coach. Roberto saluted her and the coach rolled off.

Manuel and Roberto returned by the San Isidro highway.

The sky was still overcast; the air dry; the procession of beggars was advancing in the direction of Madrid. Before they reached the Toledo Bridge, at the intersection of the San Isidro highway and the Extremadura cartroad, Roberto and Manuel entered a very large tavern. Roberto ordered a bottle of beer.

"Do you live in the same house where the shoe shop is?" asked Roberto.

"No. I live over in the Paseo de las Acacias, in a house called El Corraln."

"Good. I'll come to visit you there, and you already understand that whenever you happen to go to any place where poor folk or criminals gather, you're to let me know."

"I'll let you know. I was watching that blonde eye you. She's pretty."

"Yes."

"And she has a swell coach."

"I should say so."

"Well? Are you going to marry her?"

"What do I know? We'll see. Come, we can't stay here," said Roberto, stepping up to the counter to pay.

In the tavern a large number of beggars, seated at the tables, were gulping down slices of cod and scraps of meat; a piquant odour of fried bird-tripe and oil came from the kitchen.

They left. The wind still blew in eddies of sand; dry leaves and stray bits of newspaper danced madly through the air; the high houses near the Segovia Bridge, their narrow windows and galleries hung with tatters, seemed greyer and more sordid than ever when glimpsed through an atmosphere murky with dust.

Suddenly Roberto halted, and placing his hand upon Manuel's shoulder said:

"Listen to what I say, for it is the truth. If you ever want to accomplish anything in life, place no belief in the word 'impossible.' There's nothing impossible to an energetic will. If you try to shoot an arrow, aim very high,—as high as you can; the higher you aim, the farther you'll go."

Manuel stared at Roberto with a puzzled look, and shrugged his shoulders.

CHAPTER IV

Life In the Cobbler's Shop—Manuel's Friends.

The months of September and October were very hot; it was impossible to breathe in the shoe shop.

Every morning Manuel and Vidal, on their way to the shoemaker's, would talk of a thousand different things and exchange impressions; money, women, plans for the future formed everlasting themes of their chats. To both it seemed a great sacrifice, something in the nature of a crowning misfortune in their bad luck, to have to spend day after day cooped up in a corner ripping off outworn soles.

The languorous afternoons invited to slumber. After lunch especially, Manuel would be overcome by stupor and deep depression. Through the doorway of the shop could be seen the fields of San Isidro bathed in light; in the Campillo de Gil Imn the wash hung out to dry gleamed in the sun.

There came a medley of crowing cocks, far-off shouts of vendors, the shrieking of locomotive whistles muffled by the distance. The dry, burning, atmosphere vibrated. A few women of the neighbourhood came out to comb their hair in the open, and the mattress-makers beat their wool in the shade of the Campillo, while the hens scampered about and scratched the soil.

Later, as evening fell, the air and the earth changed to a dusty grey. In the distance, cutting the horizon, waved the outline of the arid field,—a simple line, formed by the gentle undulation of the hillocks,—a line like that of the landscapes drawn by children, with isolated houses and smoking chimneys. Here and there a lone patch of green grove splotched against the yellow field, which lay parched by the sun beneath a pallid sky, whitish and murky in the hot vapours rising from the earth. Not a cry, not the slightest sound rent the air.

At dusk the mist grew transparent and the horizon receded until, far in the distance, loomed the vague silhouettes of mountains not to be glimpsed by day, against the red background of the twilight.

When they left off working in the shop it was usually night. Seor Ignacio, Leandro, Manuel and Vidal would turn down the road toward home.

The gas lights shone at intervals in the dusty air; lines of carts rumbled slowly by, and across the road, in little groups, tramped the workmen from the neighbouring factories.

And always, coming and going, the conversation between Manuel and Vidal would turn upon the same topics: women and money.

Neither had a romantic notion, or anything like it, of women. To Manuel, a woman was a magnificent animal with firm flesh and swelling breast.

Vidal did not share this sexual enthusiasm; he experienced, with all women, a confused feeling of scorn, curiosity and preoccupation.

As far as concerned money, they were both agreed that it was the choicest, most admirable of all things; they spoke of money— especially Vidal—with a fierce enthusiasm. To him, the thought that there might be anything—good or evil—that could not be obtained with hard cash, was the climax of absurdity. Manuel would like to have money to travel all over the world and see cities and more cities and sail in vessels. Vidal's dream was to live a life of ease in Madrid.

After two or three months in the Corraln, Manuel had become so accustomed to the work and the life there that he wondered how he could do anything else. Those wretched quarters no longer produced upon him the impression of dark, sinister sadness that they cause in one unaccustomed to live in them; on the contrary, they seemed to him filled with attractions. He knew almost everybody in the district. Sundays they would meet Bizco at the Casa del Cabrero and go off into the environs: to Las Injurias, Las Cambroneras, the restaurants of Alarcn, the Campamento, and the inns on the Andaluca road, where they would consort with thieves and rogues and play with them at *can* and *rayuela*.

Manuel did not care for Bizco's company; Bizco sought only to hobnob with thieves. He was forever taking Manuel and Vidal to haunts frequented by bandits and low types, but since Vidal seemed to think it all right, Manuel never objected.

Vidal was the link between Manuel and Bizco, Bizco hated Manuel, who in turn, not only felt enmity and repugnance for Bizco, but showed this repulsion plainly. Bizco was a brute,—an animal deserving of extermination. As lascivious as a monkey, he had violated several of the little girls of the Casa del Cabrero, beating them into submission; he used to rob his father, a poverty-stricken cane-weaver, so that he might have money enough to visit some low brothel of Las Penuelas or on Chopa Street, where he found rouged dowagers with cigarette-stubs in their lips, who looked like princesses to him. His narrow skull, his powerful jaw, his blubber-lip, his stupid glance, lent him a look of repellant brutality and animality.

A primitive man, he kept his dagger—bought in El Rastro—sharp, guarding it as a sacred object. If he ever happened across a cat or dog, he would enjoy torturing it to death with oft-repeated stabs. His speech was obscene, abounding in barbarities and blasphemies.

Whether anybody induced Bizco to tattoo his arms, or the idea was original with him, cannot be said; probably the tattooing he had seen on one of the bandits that he ran after had suggested a similar adornment for himself. Vidal imitated him, and for a time the pair gave themselves up enthusiastically to self-tattooing. They pricked their skins with a pin until a little blood came, then moistened the wounds with ink.

66

Bizco painted crosses, stars and names upon his chest; Vidal, who didn't like to prick himself, stippled his own name on one arm and his sweetheart's on the other; Manuel didn't care to inscribe anything upon his person, first because he was afraid of blood, and then because the idea had been Bizco's.

Each harboured a mute hostility against the other.

Manuel, always with a chip on his shoulder, was disposed to show his enemy challenge; Bizco, doubtless, noticed this scornful hatred in Manuel's eyes, and this confused him.

To Manuel, a man's superiority consisted in his talent, and, above all, in his cunning; to Bizco, courage and strength constituted the sole enviable qualities; the greatest merit of all was to be a real brute, as he would declare with enthusiasm.

Because of the great esteem in which he held craft and cunning, Manuel felt deep admiration for the Rebolledos, father and son, who also lived in the Corraln. The father, a dwarfed hunchback, a barber by trade, used to shave his customers in the sunlight of the open, near the Rastro. This dwarf had a very intelligent face, with deep eyes; he wore moustache and side-whiskers, and long, bluish, unwashed hair. He dressed always in mourning; in winter and summer alike he went around in an overcoat, and, by some unsolved mystery of chemistry his overcoat kept turning green while his trousers, which were also black, kept quite as plainly turning red.

Every morning Rebolledo would leave the Corraln carrying a little bench and a wooden wall-bracket, from which hung a brass basin and a poster. Reaching a certain spot along the Americas fence he would attach the bracket and put up, beside it, a humorous sign the point of which, probably, he was the only one to see. It ran thus:

MODERNIST TONSORIAL PARLOUR
Antiseptic Barber
Walk in Gents. Shaving by Rebolledo.
Money Lent

The Rebolledos were very skilful; they made toys of wire and of pasteboard, which they afterward sold to the street-vendors; their home, a dingy little room of the front patio, had been converted into a workshop, and they had there a vise, a carpenter's bench and an array of broken gew-gaws that were apparently of no further use.

The neighbours of the Corraln had a saying that indicated their conception of Rebolledo's acute genius.

"That dwarf," they said, "has a regular Noah's ark in his head."

The father had made for his own use a set of false teeth. He had taken a bone napkin-ring, cut it into two unequal parts, and, by filing it on either side, had fitted the larger to his mouth. Then with a tiny saw he made the teeth, and to simulate the gums he covered a part of the former napkin-ring with sealing-wax. Rebolledo could remove and insert the false set with remarkable ease, and he could eat with them perfectly, provided, as he said, there was anything to eat.

Perico, the son of the dwarf, promised even to outstrip his father in cleverness. Between the hunger that he often suffered, and the persistent tertian fevers, he was very thin and his complexion was citreous. He was not, like his father, deformed, but slender, delicate, with sparkling eyes and rapid, jerky motions. He looked, as the saying is, like a rat under a bowl.

One of the proofs of his inventive genius was a mechanical snuffler that he had made of a shoe-polish tin.

Perico cherished a particular enthusiasm for white walls, and wherever he discovered one he would sketch, with a piece of coal, processions of men, women and horses, houses puffing smoke, soldiers, vessels at sea, weaklings engaging in struggle with burly giants, and other equally diverting scenes.

Perico's masterpiece was the Don Tancredo triptych, done in coal on the walls of the narrow entrance lane to La Corrala. This work overwhelmed the neighbours with admiration and astonishment.

The first part of the triptych showed the valiant hypnotizer of bulls on his way to the bull-ring, in the midst of a great troop of horsemen; the legend read: "Don Tancredo on his *weigh* to the bulls." The second part represented the "king of bravery" in his three-cornered hat, with his arms folded defiantly before the wild beast; underneath, the rubric "Don Tancredo upon his pedestal." Under the third part one read: "The bull takes to flight." The depiction of this final scene was noteworthy; the bull was seen fleeing as one possessed of the devil amidst the toreros, whose noses were visible in profile while their mouths and both eyes were drawn in front view.

Despite his triumphs, Perico Rebolledo did not grow vain, nor did he consider himself superior to the men of his generation; his greatest pleasure was to sit down at his father's side in the patio of La Corrala, amidst the works of old clocks, bunches of keys and other grimy, damaged articles, and ponder over the possible utilization of an eye-glass crystal, for example, or a truss, or the rubber bulb of a syringe, or some similar broken, out-of-order contrivance.

Father and son spent their lives dreaming of mechanical contraptions; they considered nothing useless; the key that could open no door, the old-style coffee-pot, as queer as some laboratory instrument, the oil lamp with machine attachment,—all these articles were treasured up, taken apart and put to some use. Rebolledo, father and son, wasted more ingenuity in living wretchedly than is employed by a couple of dozen comic authors, journalists and state ministers dwelling in luxury.

Among the friends of Perico Rebolledo were the Aristas, who became intimate with Manuel.

The Aristas, two brothers, sons of an ironing-woman, were apprentices in a foundry of the near-by Ronda. The younger passed his days in a continuous capering, indulging in death-defying leaps, climbing trees, walking on his hands and performing acrobatic stunts from all the door transoms.

The elder brother, a long-legged stutterer whom they called Aristn in jest, was the most funereal fellow on the planet; he suffered from acute necromania; anything connected with coffins, corpses, wakes and candles roused his enthusiasm. He would like to have been a gravedigger, the priest of a religious confraternity, a cemetery warden; but his great dream,—what most enchanted him,—was a funeral; he would imagine, as a wonderful ideal, the conversations that the proprietor of a funeral establishment must have with the father or the inconsolable widow as he offered wreaths of immortelles, or as he went to take the measure of a corpse or strolled amidst the coffins. What a splendid existence, this manufacturing of last resting-places for men, women and children, and afterward accompanying them to the burial-ground. For Aristn, details relating to death were the most important matter in life.

Through that irony of fate which almost always exchanges the proper labels of things and persons, Aristn was a supernumerary in one of the vaudeville theatres, through the influence of his father, who was a scene-shifter, and the job disgusted him, for in such a playhouse nobody ever died upon the stage, nobody ever came out in mourning and there was no weeping. And while Aristn kept thinking of nothing but funereal scenes, his brother dreamed of circuses, trapezes and acrobats, hoping that some day fate would send him the means to cultivate his gymnastic talents.

CHAPTER V

La Blasa's Tavern.

The frequent quarrels between Leandro and his sweetheart, the Corrector's daughter, very often gave the neighbours of the Corrala food for gossip. Leandro was an ill-tempered, quarrelsome sort; his brutal instincts were quickly awakened; despite his habit of going every Saturday night to the taverns and restaurants, ready for a rumpus with the bullies and the ruffians, he had thus far managed to steer clear of any disagreeable accident. His sweetheart was somewhat pleased with this display of valour; her mother, however, regarded it with genuine indignation, and was forever advising her daughter to dismiss her Leandro for good.

The girl would dismiss her lover; but afterwards, when he returned in humility, ready to accede to any conditions, she relented.

This confidence in her power turned the girl despotic, whimsical, voluble; she would amuse herself by rousing Leandro's jealousy; she had arrived at a particular state, a blend of affection and hatred, in which the affection remained within and the hatred outside, revealing itself in a ferocious cruelty, in the satisfaction of mortifying her lover constantly.

"What you ought to do some fine day," Seor Ignacio would say to Leandro, incensed by the cruel coquetry of the maiden, "is to get her into a corner and take all you want.... And then give her a beating and leave her soft as mush. The next day she'd be following you around like a dog."

Leandro, as brave as any bully, was as meek as a charity-pupil in the presence of his sweetheart. At times he recalled his father's counsel, but he would never have summoned the courage to carry it through.

One Saturday afternoon, after a bitter dispute with Milagros, Leandro invited Manuel to make the rounds that night together with him.

"Where'll we go?" asked Manuel.

"To the Naranjeros caf, or to the Engrima restaurant."

"Wherever you please."

"We'll make the rounds of those dives and then we'll wind up at La Blasa's tavern."

"Do the hard guys go there?"

"I should say. As tough as you make 'em."

70

"Then I'll let Roberto know,—that fellow who came for me to take him to la Doctrina."

"All right."

After work Manuel went off to the boardingrhouse and took counsel with Roberto.

"Be at the San Milln caf about nine in the evening," said Roberto, "I'll be there with a cousin of mine."

"Are you going to take her there?" Manuel asked in astonishment.

"Yes. She's a queer one, a painter."

"And is this painter good-looking?" asked Leandro.

"I can't say. I don't know her."

"Damn my sweet—— ... ! I'd give anything to have this woman come along, man."

"Me, too."

They both went to the San Milln caf, sat down and waited impatiently. At the hour indicated Roberto appeared in company of his cousin whom he called Fanny. She was a woman between thirty and forty, very slender, with a sallow complexion,—a distinguished, masculine type; there was about her something of the graceless beauty of a racehorse; her nose was curved, her jaw big, her cheeks sunken and her eyes grey and cold. She wore a jacket of dark green taffeta, a black skirt and a small hat.

Leandro and Manuel greeted her with exceeding timidity and awkwardness; they shook hands with Roberto and conversed.

"My cousin," said Roberto, "would like to see something of slum life hereabouts."

"Whenever you wish," answered Leandro. "But I warn you beforehand that there are some pretty tough specimens in this vicinity."

"Oh, I'm prepared," said the lady, with a slight foreign accent, showing a revolver of small calibre.

Roberto paid, despite Leandro's protests, and they left the caf. Coming out on the Plaza del Rastro, they walked down the Ribera de Curtidores as far as the Ronda de Toledo.

"If the lady wishes to see the house we live in, this is the one," said Leandro.

They went into the Corraln; a crowd of gamins and old women, amazed to see such a strange woman there at such an hour, surrounded them, showering Manuel and Leandro with questions. Leandro was eager for Milagros to learn that he had been there with a woman, so he accompanied Fanny through the place, pointing out all the holes of the wretched dwelling.

"Poverty's the only thing you can see here," said Leandro.

"Yes, yes indeed," answered the woman.

"Now if you wish, we'll go to La Blasa's tavern."

They left the Corraln for Embajadores lane and walked along the black fence of a laundry. It was a dark night and a drizzle had begun to fall. They stumbled along the surrounding path.

"Look-out," said Leandro. "There's a wire here."

He stepped upon the wire to hold it down. They all crossed the path and passed a group of white houses, coming to Las Injurias.

They approached a low cottage with a dark socle; a door with clouded broken panes stuffed with bundles of paper, through which shone a pallid light, gave entrance to the dwelling. In the opaque transparency of the glass appeared from time to time the shadow of a person.

Leandro opened the door and they all went in. A stuffy, smoky wave of atmosphere struck them in the face. A kerosene lamp, hanging from the ceiling and covered with a white shade, provided light for the tiny, low-roofed tavern.

As the four entered, the customers greeted them with an expression of stupefaction; for a while the habitues whispered among themselves, then some, resumed their playing as others looked on.

Fanny, Roberto, Leandro and Manuel took seats to the right of the door.

"What'll you have?" asked the woman at the counter.

"Four fifteen-cntimo glasses of wine."

The woman brought the glasses in a filthy tray, and set them upon the table. Leandro pulled out sixty cntimos.

"They're ten apiece," corrected the woman in ill-humoured tones.

"How's that?"

"Because this is outside the limits."

"All right; take whatever it comes to."

The woman left twenty cntimos on the table and returned to the counter. She was broad, large-breasted, with a head that set deep in between her shoulders and a neck composed of some five or six layers of fat; from time to time she would serve a drink, always getting the price in advance; she spoke very little, with evident displeasure and with an invariable gesture of ill-humour.

This human hippopotamus had at her right a tin tank with a spigot, for brandy, and at her left a flask of strong wine and a chipped jar covered with a black funnel, into which she poured whatever was left in the glasses by her customers.

Roberto's cousin fished out a phial of smelling salts, hid it in her clamped hand and took a sniff from time to time.

Opposite the place where Roberto, Fanny, Leandro and Manuel were seated, a crowd of some twenty men were packed around a table playing cane.

Near them, huddled on the floor next the stove, reclining against the wall, could be seen a number of ugly, scraggly-haired hags, dressed in corsages and ragged skirts that were tied around their waists by ropes.

"Who are those women?" asked the painter.

"They're old tramps," explained Leandro. "The kind that go to the Botanical Garden and the clearings outside the city."

Two or three of the unfortunates held in their arms children belonging to other women who had come there to spend the night; some were dozing with their cigarettes sticking from the corner of their mouths. Amid the old women were a few little girls of thirteen or fourteen, monstrously deformed, with bleary eyes; one of them had her nose completely eaten away, with nothing but a hole like a wound left in its place; another was hydro-cephalous, with so thin a neck that it seemed the slightest movement would snap it and send her head rolling from her shoulders.

"Have you seen the large jars they have here?" Leandro asked Manuel. "Come on and take a look."

The two rose and approached the group of gamblers. One of these interrupted his game.

"Please make way?" Leandro said to him, with marked impertinence.

The man drew in his chair sourly. There was nothing remarkable about the jars; they were large, embedded in the wall, painted with red-lead; each of them bore a sign denoting the class of wine inside, and had a spigot.

"What's so wonderful about this, I'd like to know?" asked Manuel.

Leandro smiled; they returned as they had come, disturbing the player once more and resuming their seats at the table.

Roberto and Fanny conversed in English.

"That fellow we made get up," said Leandro, "is the bully of this place."

"What's his name?" asked Fanny.

"El Valencia."

The man they were speaking about, hearing his sobriquet mentioned, turned around and eyed Leandro; for a moment their glances crossed defiantly; Valencia turned his eyes away and continued playing. He was a strong man, about forty, with high cheek bones, reddish skin and a disagreeably sarcastic expression. Every once in a while he would cast a severe look at the group formed by Fanny, Roberto and the other two.

"And that Valencia,—who is he?" asked the lady in a low voice.

"He's a mat maker by trade," answered Leandro, raising his voice. "A tramp that wheedles money out of low-lives; before he used to belong to the *pote*,—the kind that visit houses on Sundays, knock, and when they see nobody's home, stick their jimmy into the lock and zip!... But he hasn't the courage even for this, 'cause his liver is whiter than paper."

"It would be curious to investigate," said Roberto, "just how far poverty has served as centre of gravity for the degradation of these men."

"And how about that white-bearded old fellow at his side?" asked Fanny.

"He's one of those apostles that cure with water. They say he's a wise old fellow.... He has a cross on his tongue. But I believe he painted it there himself."

"And that other woman there?"

"That's La Paloma, Valencia's mistress."

74

"Prostitute?" asked the lady.

"For at least forty years," answered Leandro with a laugh.

They all looked closely at Paloma; she had a huge, soft face, with pouches of violet skin, and a timid look as of a humble beast; she represented at least forty years of prostitution and all its concomitant ills; forty years of nights spent in the open, lurking about barracks, sleeping in suburban shanties and the most repulsive lodgings.

Among the women there was also a gypsy who, from time to time, would get up and walk across the tavern with a saucy strut.

Leandro ordered some glasses of whiskey; but it was so bad that nobody could drink it.

"Hey, you," called Leandro to the gipsy, offering her the glass. "Want a drink?"

"No."

The gypsy placed her hands upon the table,—a pair of stubby, wrinkled hands incrusted with dirt.

"Who are these gumps?" she asked Leandro.

"Friends of mine. Will you drink or not?" and he offered her the glass again.

"No."

Then in a shrill voice, he shouted:

"Apostle, will you have a drink?"

The Apostle rose from his place amongst the gamblers. He was dead drunk and could hardly move; his eyes were viscous, like those of an angered animal; he staggered over to Leandro and took the glass, which trembled in his grasp; he brought it to his lips and gulped it down.

"Want more?" asked the gypsy.

"Sure, sure," he drooled.

Then he began to babble, showing the stumps of his yellow teeth, but nobody could understand a word; he drained the other glasses, rested his forehead against his hand

and slowly made his way to a corner, into which he squatted, and then stretched himself out on the floor.

"Do you want me to tell your fortune, princess?" asked the gipsy of Fanny, seizing her hand.

"No," replied the lady drily.

"Won't you give me a few coins for the *churumbeles*?"

"No."

"Wicked woman! Why won't you give me a few coins for the *churumbeles*?"

"What does *churumbeles* mean?" asked the lady.

"Her children," answered Leandro, laughing.

"Have you children?" Fanny asked the gipsy.

"Yes."

"How many?"

"Two. Here they are."

And the gipsy fetched a blond little fellow and a girl of about five or six.

The lady petted the little boy; then she took a duro from her purse and gave it to the gipsy.

The gipsy, parting her lips in amazement and bursting forth into profuse flattery, exhibited the duro to everybody in the place.

"We'd better be going," advised Leandro. "To pull one of those big coins out in a dive like this is dangerous."

The four left the tavern.

"Would you like to make the rounds of this quarter?" asked Leandro.

"Yes. Let's," said the lady.

Together they wound in and out of the narrow lanes of Las Injurias.

76

"Watch out, the drain runs in the middle of the street," cautioned Manuel.

The rain kept falling; the quartet of slummers entered narrow patios where their feet sank into the pestiferous slime. Along the entire extension of the ravine black with mud, shone but a single oil lamp, attached to the side of some half crumbled wall.

"Shall we go back?" asked Roberto.

"Yes," answered the lady.

They set out for Embajadores lane and walked up the Paseo de las Acacias. The rain came down harder; here and there a faint light shone in the distance; against the intense darkness of the sky loomed the vague silhouette of a high chimney....

Leandro and Manuel accompanied Fanny and Roberto as far as the Plaza del Rastro, and there they parted, exchanging handshakes.

"What a woman!" exclaimed Leandro.

"Nice, eh?" asked Manuel.

"You bet. I'd give anything to have a try at her."

CHAPTER VI

Roberto In Quest of a Woman—El Tabuenca and his Inventions—Don
Alonso or the Snake-Man.

A few months later Roberto appeared in the Corrala at the hour when Manuel and the
shoe-shop employs were returning from their day's work.

"Do you know Seor Zurro?" Roberto asked Manuel.

"Yes. He lives here on this side."

"I know that. I'd like to have a talk with him.

"Then knock at his door. He must be in."

"Come along with me."

Manuel knocked and Encarna opened; they went inside. Seor Zurro was in his room,
reading a newspaper by the light of a large candle; the place was a regular
storehouse, cluttered with old secretaries, dilapidated chests, mantlepieces, clocks
and sundry other items. It was close enough to stifle a person; it was impossible to
breathe or to take a step without stumbling against something.

"Are you Seor Zurro?" asked Roberto.

"Yes."

"I have come at the suggestion of Don Telmo."

"Don Telmo!" repeated the old man, rising and offering the student a chair. "Have a
seat. How is the good gentleman?"

"Very well."

"He's an excellent friend of mine," continued Zurro. "I should say so. Well, young
man, let me know what you wish. It's enough for me that you come from Don
Telmo; that assures you my best services."

"I should like to learn the whereabouts of a certain girl acrobat who lived about five
or six years ago in a lodging-house of this vicinity, or in Cuco's hostelry."

"And do you know this girl's name?"

"Yes."

"And you say that she used to live in Cuco's hostelry?"

"Yes, sir."

"I know somebody who lives there," murmured the second-hand dealer.

"Yes, that's so," said Encarna.

"That man with the monkeys. Didn't he live there?" asked Seor Zurro.

"No; he lived in la Quinta de Goya," answered his daughter.

"Well, then.... Just wait a moment, young man. Wait a moment."

"Isn't it Tabuenca that lives there, father?" interrupted Encarna.

"That's the fellow. That's it. El Tabuenca. You go and see him. And tell him," added Seor Zurro, turning to Roberto, "that I sent you. He's a grouchy old fellow, as testy as they make 'em."

Roberto took leave of the second-hand man and his daughter, and in company of Manuel walked out to the gallery of the house.

"And where's this Cuco's hostelry?" he asked.

"Over there near Las Yeseras," answered Manuel.

"Come along with me, then; we'll have supper together," suggested Roberto.

"All right."

They both went on to the hostelry, which was situated upon a thoroughfare that was deserted at this hour. It was a large building, with an entrance-vestibule in country style and a patio crowded with carts. They questioned a boy. El Tabuenca had just come, he told them. They walked into the vestibule, which was illuminated by a lantern. There was a man inside.

"Does anybody live here by the name of Tabuenca?" asked Roberto.

"Yes. What is it?" asked the man.

"I'd like to have a talk with him."

"Well, talk away, then, for I'm Tabuenca."

As the speaker turned, the light of the oil lantern hanging upon the wall struck him full in the face; Roberto and Manuel stared at him in amazement. He was a yellow, shrivelled specimen; he had an absurd nose, as if it had been wrenched from its roots and replaced by a round little ball of meat. It seemed that he looked at the same time with his eyes and with the two little nasal orifices. He was clean-shaven, dressed pretty decently, and wore a round woollen cap with a green visor.

He listened grumpily to what Roberto had to say; then he lighted a cigar and flung the match far away. Doubtless because of the exiguity of his organ, he found it necessary to stop the windows of his nose with his fingers in order to smoke.

Roberto thought at first that the man had not understood his question, and he repeated it twice. Tabuenca gave no heed; but all at once, seized with the utmost indignation, he snatched the cigar furiously from his mouth and began to blaspheme in a whining, gull-like voice, shrieking that he couldn't make out why folks pestered him with matters that didn't concern him a particle.

"Don't shout so," said Roberto, provoked by this rumpus. "They'll imagine that we've come here to assassinate you, at the very least."

"I shout because I please to."

"All right, man; shout away to your heart's content."

"Don't you talk to me like that or I'll push in your face," yelled Tabuenca.

"*You'll* push in *my* face?" retorted Roberto, laughing; then, turning to Manuel, he added, "These noseless fellows get on my nerves and I'm going to let this flat-nose have it."

Tabuenca, his mind made up, withdrew and returned in a short while with a rapier-cane, which he unsheathed; Roberto looked in every direction for something with which he might defend himself, and found a carter's stick; Tabuenca aimed a thrust at Roberto, who parried it with the stick; then another thrust, and Roberto, as again he parried it, smashed the lantern at the entrance, leaving the scene in darkness. Roberto began to strike out right and left and he must have landed once upon some delicate part of Tabuenca's anatomy, for the man began to shout in horrible tones:

"Assassins! Murder!"

At this, several persons came running into the zagun, among them a stout mule-driver with an oil-lamp in his hand.

80

"What's the trouble?" he asked.

"These murderers are after my life," bellowed Tabuenca.

"Not a bit of it," replied Roberto in a calm voice. "The fact is, we came here to ask this fellow a civil question, and without any reason at all he began to yell and insult me."

"I'll smash your face for you!" interjected Tabuenca.

"Well suppose you try it, and don't stand there talking all day about it!" Roberto taunted,

"Rascal! Coward!"

"It's you who are the coward. You've got as little guts as you have nose."

Tabuenca spat out a series of insults and blasphemies, and turning around, left the place.

"And who's going to pay me for this broken lantern?" asked the mule-driver.

"How much is it worth?" asked Roberto.

"Three pesetas."

"Here they are."

"That Tabuenca is a loud-mouthed imbecile," said the mule-driver as he took the money. "And what was it you gentlemen wished?"

"I wanted to ask about a woman that lived here some years ago; she was an acrobat."

"Perhaps Don Alonso, Titiri, would know. If you'll be so kind, tell me where you're going, and I'll have Titiri look you up."

"All right. You tell him that we'll be waiting for him at the San Milln caf at nine o'clock," said Roberto.

"And how are we going to recognize this fellow?" asked Manuel.

"That's so," said Roberto. "How are we going to know him?"

"Easy. He goes around nights through the cafs with one of those apparatuses that sings songs."

"You mean a phonograph?"

"That's it."

At this juncture an old woman appeared in the entrance, shouting:

"Who was the dirty son of a bitch that broke the lantern?"

"Shut up, shut up," answered the mule-driver. "It's all paid for."

"Come along!" said Manuel to Roberto.

They left the inn and strode off at a fast clip. They entered the San Milln caf. Roberto ordered supper. Manuel knew Tabuenca from having seen him in the street, and as they ate he explained to Roberto just what sort of fellow he was.

Tabuenca made his living through a number of inventions that he himself constructed. When he saw that the public was tiring of one thing, he would put another on the market, and so he managed to get along. One of these contraptions was a wafer-mold wheel that revolved around a circle of nails among which numbers were inscribed and colours painted. This wheel the owner carried about in a pasteboard box with two covers, which were divided into tiny squares with numbers and colours corresponding to those placed around the nails, and here the bets were laid. Tabuenca would carry the closed box in one hand and a field table in the other. He would set up his outfit at some street corner, give the wheel a turn and begin to mutter in his whining voice;

"'Round goes the wheel. Place your bets, gentlemen.... Place your bets. Number or colour ... number or colour.... Place your bets."

When enough bets were placed,—and this happened fairly often,—Tabuenca would set the wheel spinning, at the same time repeating his slogan: "'Round goes the wheel!" The marble would bounce amidst the nails and even before it came to a stop the operator knew the winning number and colour, crying: "Red seven...." or "the blue five," and always he guessed right.

As Manuel spoke on, Roberto became pensive.

"Do you see?" he said, all at once, "these delays are what provoke a fellow. You have a capital of will in bank-notes, gold-pieces, in large denominations, and you need energy in cntimos, in small change. It's the same with the intelligence; that's why so many intelligent and energetic men of ambition do not succeed. They lack

82

fractions, and in general they also lack the talent to conceal their efforts. To be able to be stupid on some occasions would probably be more useful than the ability to be discreet on just as many other occasions."

Manuel, who did not understand the reason for this shower of words, stared open-mouthed at Roberto, who sank again into his meditations.

For a long time both remained silent, when there came into the caf a tall, thin man with greyish hair and grey moustache.

"Can that be Titiri, Don Alonso?" asked Roberto.

"Maybe."

The gaunt fellow went from table to table, exhibiting a box and announcing: "Here's a novelty. Here's somethin' new."

He was about to leave when Roberto called him.

"Do you live at Cuco's hostelry?" he asked.

"Yes, sir."

"Are you Don Alonso?"

"At your service."

"Well, we've been waiting for you. Take a seat; you'll have coffee with us."

The man took a seat. His appearance was decidedly comical,—a blend of humility, bragodoccio and sad arrogance. He gazed at the place that Roberto had just abandoned, in which remained a scrap of roast meat.

"Pardon me," he said to Roberto. "You're not intending to finish that scrap? No? Then.... with your permission—" and he took the plate, the knife and the fork.

"I'll order another beefsteak for you," said Roberto.

"No, no. It's one of my whims. I imagine that this meat must be good. Would you kindly let me have a slice of bread?" he added, turning to Manuel. "Thanks, young man. Many thanks."

The man bolted the meat and bread in a trice.

"What? Is there a little wine left?" he asked, smiling.

"Yes," replied Manuel, emptying the bottle into the man's glass.

"All right," answered the man in ill-pronounced English as he gulped it down. "Gentlemen! At your service. I believe you wished to ask me something."

"Yes."

"At your service, then. My name is Alonso de Guzmn Caldern y Tllez. This same fellow that's talking to you now has been director of a circus in America; I've travelled through all the countries and sailed over every sea in the world; at present I'm adrift in a violent tempest; at night I go from caf to caf with this phonograph, and the next morning I carry around one of thcsc betting apparatuses that consists of an *Infiel*[1] Tower with a spiral. Underneath the tower there's a space with a spring that shoots a little bone ball up the spiral, and then the bone falls upon a board perforated with holes and painted in different colours. That is my livelihood. I! Director of an equestrian circus! This is what I've descended to; an assistant to Tabuenca. What things come to pass in this world!"

[Footnote 1: *i.e.* Faithless. A pun on Eiffel.]

"I should like to ask you," interrupted Roberto, "if during your residence in Cuco's hostelry you ever made the acquaintance of a certain Rosita Buenavida, a circus acrobat."

"Rosita Buenavida! You say that her name was Rosita Buenavida?... No, I don't recall.... I did have a Rosita in my company; but her name wasn't Buenavida (i. e., Goodlife); she'd have been better named Evil-life and evil habits, too."

"Perhaps she changed her name," said Roberto impatiently. "What age was the Rosita that you knew?"

"Well, I'll tell you; I was in Paris in '68; had a contract with the Empress Circus. At that time I was a contortionist and they called me the Snake-Man; then I became an equilibrist and adopted the name of Don Alonso. Alonso is my name. After four months of that Prez and I—Prez was the greatest gymnast in the world—went to America, and two or three years later we met Rosita, who must have been about twenty-five or thirty at that time."

"So that the Rosita you're talking about should be sixty-odd years old today," computed Roberto. "The one I'm looking for can't be more than thirty at most."

"Then she's not the one. Caramba, how sorry I am!" murmured Don Alonso, seizing the glass of coffee and milk and raising it to his lips as if he feared it were going to

84

be wrested from him. "And what a sweet little girl she was! She had eyes as green as a cat's. Oh, she was a pretty chit, a peach."

Roberto had sunk into meditation; Don Alonso continued his chatter, turning to Manuel:

"There's no life like a circus artist's," he exclaimed. "I don't know what your profession is, and I don't want to disparage it; but if you're looking for art.... Ah, Paris, the Empress Circus,—I'll never forget them! Of course, Prez and I had luck; we created a furore there, and I needn't mention what that means. Oh, that was the life.... Nights, after our performance, we'd get a note: 'Will be waiting for you at such and such a caf.' We'd go there and find one of your high-life women, a whimsical creature who'd invite a fellow to supper... and to all the rest. But other gymnasts came to the Empress Circus; the novelty of our act wore off, and the impresario, a Yankee who owned several companies, asked Prez and me if we wanted to go to Cuba. 'Right ahead,' said I. 'All right.'"

"Have you been in Cuba?" asked Roberto, roused from his abstraction.

"I've been in so many places!" replied the Snake-Man. "We embarked at Havre," continued Don Alonso, "on a vessel called the Navarre, and we were in Havana for about eight months; while we were performing there we struck it big, Prez and I, and won twenty thousand gold pesos in the lottery."

"Twenty thousand duros!" exclaimed Manuel.

"Right-o! The next week we had lost it all, and Prez and I were left without a centavo. A few days we lived on guava-fruit and yam, until we fell in with some gymnasts on the Havana wharf who were down on their uppers. We joined them. They weren't at all bad performers; among them were acrobats, clowns, pantominists, bar artists, and a French ecuyre; we formed a company and made a tour through the island towns; and some magnificent tour that was. How they did welcome us and treat us in that country! 'Come right in, friend, and have a glass.' 'Many thanks.' 'The gentleman mustn't displease me; let's have a drink in that cantine, eh? ...' And the drink flowed to your heart's content. As I was the only one in the troupe that knew how to figure—for I've had an education," interposed Don Alonso, "and my father was a soldier—they named me director. In one of the towns I reinforced the company with a ballerina and a strong man. The dancer's name was Rosita Montas; she's the one I thought of when you mentioned the Rosita you were looking for. This Montas was Spanish and had married the strong man, an Italian whose real name was Napoleon Pitti. The couple had with them as secretary a Galician,—very intelligent chap, but as an artist, detestable. And between Rosita and him they deceived Hercules. This wasn't very hard, for Napoleon was one of the ugliest men I've ever laid eyes on. As for strength, there was never his match; he had a back as solid as a front wall; his ears were flattened from blows got in prize-fighting; he was a barbarian for fair, and you know what they say: 'Tell a man by his talk and a bullock by his horn.' And believe me, this little Galician chap led

Hercules by the horn, all right. The cursed smarty fooled me, too, though not as he did Hercules, for I've always been a bachelor, thank the Lord, partly through fear and partly through design. Nor have I ever lacked women," added Don Alonso, boastfully.

"What was I saying, now? Oh, yes. I didn't know any English; the damned lingo isn't very hard, but I simply couldn't get it into my head. So I needed an interpreter, and I appointed the Galician as secretary of the company and ticket-seller. We had been together for almost a year when we reached an English island near Jamaica. The governor of the island, the queerest Englishman there ever was, with a pair of side-whiskers that looked like flames leaping from his cheeks, summoned me as soon as we landed. As there was no site for our performances, he made alterations in the municipal school, which was a regular palace; he ordered all the partitions removed and the ring and tiers of seats installed. Only the negroes of the town went to that school, and what need had those creatures of learning to read and write?

"We stayed there a month, and despite the fact that we had rent free and that we played to full houses every afternoon, and that we had practically no expenses, we didn't make any profit. 'How can it be?' I kept asking myself.—A mystery."

"And what was the reason?" asked Manuel.

"I'm coming to that. First I must explain that the governor with the flaming side-whiskers had fallen in love with Rosita, and without beating around the bush he had taken her off to his palace. Poor Hercules roared and crushed the dishes with his fingers, drowning his grief and his rage by committing all sorts of barbarities.

"The governor, a generous sort, invited the Galician and me to his residence, and there, in a garden of cedars and palms, we would draw up the program of the performances, and amuse ourselves at target-practice while we smoked the finest tobacco and drank glass after glass of rum. We paid court to Rosita and she'd laugh like a madwoman, and dance the tango, the *cachucha* and the *vito*, and she'd fail the Englishman an awful number of times. One day the governor, who treated me as a friend, said to me: 'That secretary of yours is robbing you.' 'I think he is,' I answered. 'Tonight you'll have the proof.'

"We finished the performance; I went off home, had supper and was about to go to bed when a little negro servant comes in and tells me to follow him; all right; I follow; we both leave; we draw near the circus house, and in a nearby saloon I see the governor and the town chief of police. It was a very beautiful moonlit night, and there was no light in the saloon; we wait and wait, and soon a figure appears, and steals in through a window of the schoolhouse. '*Forwer*' whispered the governor. That means Forward," interpreted Don Alonso.

"The three of us followed and entered noiselessly through the same window; on tiptoe we reached the entrance to the former school, which served as the circus vestibule and contained the ticket-office. We see the secretary with a lantern in his

86

hand going through the money-box. 'Surrender in the name of the authorities!' shouted the governor, and with the revolver that he held in his hand he fired a shot into the air. The secretary was paralyzed at the sight of us; then the governor aimed the gun at the fellow's chest and fired again point blank; and the man wavered, turned convulsively in the air and fell dead.

"The governor was jealous and the truth is that Rosita was in love with the secretary. I never in my life saw grief as great as that woman's when she found her lover dead. She wept and dragged along after him, uttering wails that simply tore your soul in two. Napoleon, too, wept.

"We buried the secretary and four or five days later the chief of police of the island informed us that the school could no longer serve as a circus and that we'd have to clear out. We obeyed the order, for there was no way out of it, and for another couple of years we wandered from town to town through Central America, Yucatan, Mexico, until we struck Tampico, where the company disbanded. As there was no outlook for us there, Prez and I took a vessel for New Orleans."

"Beautiful town, eh?" said Roberto.

"Beautiful. Have you been there?"

"Yes."

"Man, how happy I am to hear it!"

"What a river, eh?"

"An ocean! Well, to continue my story. The first time we performed in that city, gentlemen, what a success! The circus was higher than a church; I said to the carpenter; 'Place our trapeze as high as possible,' and after giving him these orders I went off for a bite.

"During our absence the impresario happened along and asked: 'Are those Spanish gymnasts going to perform at such a height?' 'That's what they said,' answered the carpenter. 'Let them know, then, that I don't want to be responsible for such barbarity.'

"Prez and I were in the hotel, when we received a message calling us to the circus at once."

"'What can it be?' my companion asked me. 'You'll see,' I told him. 'They're going to demand that we lower the trapeze.'

"And so it was. Prez and I go to the circus and we see the impresario. That was what he requested.

"'Nothing doing,' I told him. 'Not even if the President of the Republic of the United States himself comes here, together with his esteemed mother. I won't lower the trapeze an inch.' 'Then you'll be compelled to.' 'We'll see.' The impresario summoned a policeman; I showed the fellow my contract, and he sided with me; he told me that my companion and I had a perfect right to break our necks...."

"What a country!" murmured Roberto, ironically.

"You're right," agreed Don Alonso in all seriousness. "What a country. That's what you call progress!

"That night, in the circus, before we went on, Prez and I listened to the comments of the public. 'What? Are these Spaniards going to perform at such an altitude?' the people were asking each other. 'They'll kill themselves.' And we listened calmly, all the time smiling.

"We were about to enter the ring, when along comes a fellow with sailor's chinwhiskers wearing a flat-brimmed high hat and a carrick, and in a twanging voice he tells us that we're in danger of having a terrible accident performing 'way up there, and that, if we wish, we can take out life insurance. All we'd have to do is to sign a few papers that he had in his hand. Lord! I nearly died. I felt like choking the fellow.

"Trembling and screwing up our courage, Prez and I entered the ring. We had to put on a little rouge. We wore a blue costume decorated with silver stars,—a reference to the United States flag; we saluted and then, up the rope.

"At first I thought that I was going to slip; my head was going 'round, my ears were humming; but with the first applause I forgot everything, and Prez and I performed the most difficult feats with most admirable precision. The public applauded wildly. What days those were!"

And the old gymnast smiled; then he made a bitter grimace; his eyes grew moist; he blinked so as to dry a tear that at last escaped and coursed down his earth-coloured cheek.

"I'm an old fool; but I can't help it," Don Alonso murmured in explanation of his weakness.

"And did you stay in New Orleans?" asked Roberto.

"Prez and I signed a contract there," replied Don Alonso, "with a big circus syndicate of New York that had about twenty or thirty companies touring all

America. All of us gymnasts, ballet-dancers, ecuyres, acrobats, pantominists, clowns, contortionists, and strong men travelled in a special train.... The majority were Italians and Frenchmen."

"Were there good-looking women, eh?" asked Manuel.

"Uf! ... Like this ..." replied Don Alonso, bringing his fingers all together. "Women with such muscles! ... There was no other life anything like it," he added, reverting to his melancholy theme. "You had all the money and women and clothes you wanted.... And above all, glory, applause...."

And the gymnast went into a trance of enthusiasm, staring rigidly at a fixed point.

Roberto and Manuel gazed at him in curiosity.

"And Rosita,—didn't you ever see her again?" asked Roberto.

"No. They told me that she had got a divorce from Napoleon so that she could marry again, in Boston, some millionaire from the West. Ah, women.... Who can trust them? ... But gentlemen, it's already eleven. Pardon me; I'll have to be going. Thanks ever so much!" murmured Don Alonso, seizing Roberto and Manuel by the hands and pressing them effusively. "We'll meet again, won't we?"

"Oh, yes, we'll see each other," replied Roberto.

Don Alonso picked up his phonograph and wound in and out among the tables, repeating his phrase: "Novelty! Something new!" Then, after having saluted Roberto and Manuel once more, he disappeared.

"Nothing. I can't discover a thing," grumbled Roberto. "Good-bye. See you again."

Manuel was left alone, and musing upon Don Alonso's tales and upon the mystery surrounding Roberto, he returned to the Corraln and went to bed.

CHAPTER VII

The Kermesse on Pasin Street—"The Dude"—A Caf Chantant.

Leandro eagerly awaited the kermesse that was to take place on Pasin street. In former years he had accompanied Milagros to the nocturnal fair of San Antonio and to those of the Prado; he had danced with her, treated her to buns, presented her with a pot of sweet basil; but this summer the proof-reader's family seemed very much determined upon keeping Milagros away from Leandro. He had learned that his sweetheart and her mother were thinking of going to the kermesse, so he procured a pair of tickets and told Manuel that they two would attend.

So it happened. They went, on a terribly hot August night; a dense, turbid vapour filled all the streets in the vicinity of the Rastro, which were decorated and illuminated with Venetian lanterns.

The festival was celebrated upon a large vacant lot on Pasin street. Leandro and Manuel entered as the band from the Orphan Asylum was playing a *habanera*. The lot, aglare with arc-lights, was bedecked with ribbons, gauze and artificial flowers that radiated from a pole in the centre to the boundaries of the enclosure. Before the entrance door there was a tiny wooden booth adorned with red and yellow percale and a number of Spanish flags; this was the raffle stand.

Leandro and Manuel took a seat in a corner and waited. The proof-reader and his family did not arrive until after ten; Milagros looked very pretty that night; she had on a light costume with blue figuring, a kerchief of black crape and white slippers. She wore her gown somewhat decollet, as far as the smooth, round beginnings of her throat.

At this moment the band from the Orphan Asylum blared forth the schottisch called *Los Cocineros* (The Cooks). Leandro, stirred by the strains, invited Milagros out for a dance, but the maiden made a slight gesture of annoyance.

"You might soil my new costume," she murmured, and put her kerchief around her waist.

"If you dance with another fellow he'll soil it, too," replied Leandro in all humility.

Milagros did not heed his words; she danced with her skirt gathered in one hand, answering him in peevish monosyllables.

The schottisch over, Leandro invited the family to refreshments. To the right of the entrance there were two decorated staircases, which led to another lot about six or seven metres above the grounds where the dance was being held. On one of the stairways, which were both aglow with Spanish flags, was a signpost reading "Refreshments: Entrance" upon the other, "Refreshments: Exit."

They all went upstairs. The refreshment-parlour was a spacious place, with trees and illumination of electric globes that hung from thick cables. Seated at the tables was a motley crowd, speaking at the top of their voices, clapping their hands and laughing.

They had to wait a long while before a waiter brought them their beer; Milagros ordered an ice, and as there were none, she would have nothing.

She sat there thus, without opening her mouth, considering herself grievously offended, until she met two girls from her shop and joined them, whereupon her displeasure vanished in a trice. Leandro, at the first opportunity, left the proof-reader and, rejoining Manuel, set off in quest of his sweetheart. In the lot next to the entrance, where the dancing was going on, couples resting between numbers strolled around in leisurely fashion. Milagros and her two friends, arms linked, came by in jovial mood, followed closely by three men. One of them was a rough-looking youth, tall, with fair moustache; the other a stupid fellow, of ordinary appearance, with dyed moustache, shirt-front and fingers sparkling with diamonds; the third was a knave with, cheek-whiskers, half gipsy and half cattle-dealer, with every ear mark of the most dangerous mountebank.

Leandro, noticing the manoeuvres of the masculine trio, thrust himself in between the maidens and their gallants, and turning to the men impertinently asked:

"What's up?"

The trio pretended not to understand and lagged behind.

"Who are they?" asked Manuel.

"One of them's Lechuguino (the dude)," answered Leandro in a loud voice, so that his sweetheart should hear. "He's at least fifty, and he comes around here trying to play the dashing young blade; that runt with the dyed moustache is Pepe el Federal (the Federalist), and the other is Eusebio el Carnicero (the Butcher), a fellow who owns quite a number of questionable horses."

Leandro's blustering outburst appealed to one of the maidens, who turned to look at the youth and smiled at him; but Milagros was not in the least affected, and looking back, she repeatedly sought the group of three men with her glance.

At this juncture there appeared the fellow whom Leandro had designated with the sobriquet of Lechuguino, in company of the proof-reader and his wife. The three girls approached them, and Lechuguino invited Milagros to dance. Leandro glanced in anguish at his sweetheart; she, however, whirled off heedlessly. The band was playing the *pas double* from the *Drummer of the Grenadiers*. Lechuguino was an expert dancer; he swept his partner along as if she were a feather and as he spoke, brought his lips so close to hers that it seemed as if he were kissing her.

Leandro was at an utter loss and suffered agonies; he could not make up his mind to leave. The dance came to an end and Lechuguino accompanied Milagros to the place where her mother was sitting.

"Come. Let's be going!" said Leandro to Manuel. "If we don't, I'm sure to do something rash."

They escaped from the fair and entered a caf chantant on Encomienda Street. It was deserted. Two girls were dancing on a platform; one dressed like a *maja*, the other, like a *manlo*.

Leandro, absorbed in his thoughts, said nothing; Manuel was very sleepy.

"Let's get out of here," muttered Leandro after a short while. "This is too gloomy."

They walked to the Plaza del Progreso, Leandro with head bowed, as pensive as ever, and Manuel so sleepy that he could hardly stand.

"Over at the Marina caf," suggested Leandro, "there must be a high old time."

"It would be better to go home," answered Manuel.

Leandro, without listening to his companion, walked to the Puerta del Sol, and the two very silently turned into Montera Street and around the corner of Jardines. It was past one. As the pair walked on, prostitutes in their gay attire accosted them from the doorways in which they lurked, but looking into Leandro's grim countenance and Manuel's poverty-stricken features the girls let them walk on, following them with a gibe at their seriousness.

Midway up the narrow, gloomy street shone a red lamp, which illuminated the squalid front of the Marina caf.

Leandro shoved the door open and they went inside. At one end the platform, with four or five mirrors, glittered dazzlingly; the floor was so tightly jammed with rows of tables thrust against either wall that only a narrow passage was left in the middle.

Leandro and Manuel found a seat. Manuel rested his forehead against his palm and was soon asleep; Leandro beckoned to one of the two singers, who were gaily dressed and were conversing with some fat women, and the two singers sat down at his table.

"What'll you have?" asked Leandro.

"Canary-seed for me," answered one of them,—a slender, nervous type with small eyes that were ringed with cosmetics.

92

"And what's your name?"

"Mine? Mara la Chivato,"

"And that girl's?"

"La Tarugo."

Tarugo, who was a buxom, gipsy-like Malaguea, sat down beside Leandro, and they started a conversation in hushed tones.

The waiter approached.

"Let's have four whiskies," ordered Chivato. "For this chap is going to drink, too," she added, turning to Manuel and seizing his arm. "Hey, you there, lad!"

"Eh!" exclaimed the boy, waking up without a notion of his whereabouts. "What do you want?"

Chivato burst into laughter.

"Wake up, man, you'll lose your express! Did you come in this afternoon on the mixed train?"

"I came on the ..." and Manuel let loose a stream of obscenity.

Then, in very ugly humour, he began to stare in every direction, making all manner of efforts not to fall asleep.

At a table set aside a man who looked like a horse-dealer was discussing the *flamenco* song and dance with a cross-eyed fellow bearing every appearance of an assassin.

"There's no more artists," the horse-dealer was saying. "Once upon a time folks came here to see Pinto, Canito, the Feos, the Macarronas.... Now what? Now, nothing. Pullets in vinegar."

"That's what," agreed the cross-eyed assassin, very seriously.

"That's the musician," said Chivato, pointing to the latter.

The two singers did not remain very long at the table with Leandro and Manuel. The cross-eyed fellow was already on the platform; he began to tune the guitar, and six women sat down around him in a row, beginning to clap hands in time to the music; Tarugo rose from her seat and started a side dance, and was soon wiggling her hips convulsively; the singer commenced to gargarize softly; at intervals he would be silent and then nothing would be heard save the snapping of Tarugo's fingers and the clatter of her heels, which played the counterpoint.

After the Malaga singer had finished, a gipsy youth with a chocolate complexion got up and executed a tango and a negro dance; he twisted himself in and out, thrust his abdomen forward and his arms back. He wound up with effeminate undulations of his hips and a most complicated intertwining of arms and legs.

"That's what you call art!" commended! the horse-dealer.

"See here, I'm going," grumbled Manuel.

"Wait a minute; we'll have another drink."

"No. I'm going."

"All right; let's come. Too bad!"

At that moment a corpulent singer with a powerful neck, and the cross-eyed guitarist with the assassin's face, came forward to the public, and while the one strummed the guitar, suddenly muting the strings by placing his hands over them, the other, his face flushed, the veins of his neck standing out tensely, and his eyes bulging from their sockets, poured forth a guttural wail that was doubtless of most difficult execution, for it reddened him to the very forehead.

CHAPTER VIII

Leandro's Irresolution—In Blasa's Tavern—The Man With The Three
Cards—The Duel With Valencia.

Some nights Manuel would hear Leandro tossing about in his bed and heaving sighs
as deep as a bull's roar.

"Things are going rotten with him," thought Manuel.

The break between Milagros and Leandro was definitive. Lechuguino, on the other
hand, was gaining ground: he had won over the girl's mother, would treat the proof-
reader and wait for Milagros where she worked, accompanying her home.

One day, toward dusk, Manuel saw the pair near the foot of Embajadores Street;
Lechuguino minced along with his cloak thrown back across his shoulder; she was
huddled in her mantle; he was talking to her and she was laughing.

"What's Leandro going to do when he finds out?" Manuel asked himself. "No, I'm
not going to tell him. Some witch of the neighbourhood will see to it that he learns
soon enough."

And thus it came about; before a month had passed, everybody in the house knew
that Milagros and Lechuguino were keeping company, that he had given up the gay
life in the dives of the city and was considering the continuation of his father's
business,—the sale of construction material; he was going to settle down and lead
the life of a respectable member of the community.

While Leandro would be away working in the shoeshop, Lechuguino would visit the
proof-reader's family; he now saw Milagros with the full consent of her parents.

Leandro was, or pretended to be, the only person unaware of Milagros' new beau.
Some mornings as the boy passed Seor Zurro's apartment on the way down to the
patio, he would encounter Encarna, who, catching sight of him, would ask
maliciously after Milagros, or else sing him a tango which began:

Of all the crazy deeds a man commits in his life,
 The craziest is taking to himself a wife.
  (De las grandes locuras que el hombre hace,
   No comete ninguna como casarse.)

Whereupon she would specify the madness and entering into details, would add at
the top of her voice:

He's off to his office bright and early,
  While some neighbourhood swell stays at home with his girlie.
   (Y por la maana el va a la oficina,
    y ella queda en casa con algun vecino que es persona
       fina.)

Leandro's bitterness corroded the very depths of his soul, and however much he tried to dominate his instincts, he could not succeed in calming himself. One Saturday night, as they were walking homewards along the Ronda, Leandro drew near to Manuel.

"Do you know whether Milagros talks to Lechuguino?"

"I?"

"Haven't you heard that they were going to get married?"

"Yes; so folks say."

"What would you do in my case?"

"I ... I'd find out."

"And suppose it proved to be true?"

Manuel was silent. They walked along without a word. Soon Leandro carne to an abrupt stop and placed his hand upon Manuel's shoulder.

"Do you believe," he asked, "that if a woman deceives a man, he has the right to kill her?"

"I don't believe he has," answered Manuel, staring into Leandro's eyes.

"Well, if a man has the guts he does it whether he has a right to or not.

"But, the deuce! Has Milagros deceived you? Were you married to her? You've had a quarrel; that's all."

"I'll wind up by doing something desperate. Take my word for it," muttered Leandro.

Neither spoke. They entered La Corrala, climbed up the stairways and walked into Leandro's house. They brought out supper, but Leandro didn't eat; he drank three glasses of water in succession and went out to the gallery.

Manuel was about to leave after supper, when he heard Leandro call him several times.

"What do you want?"

"Come on, let's be going."

Manuel ran out to the balcony; Milagros and her mother, from their door, were heaping insults upon Leandro.

"Outcast! Blackguard!" the proof-reader's wife was shouting. "If her father were here you wouldn't talk like that."

"I would, too, even if her grandfather were here," exclaimed Leandro, with a savage laugh. "Come on, let's be off," he added, turning to Manuel. "I'm sick and tired of these whores."

They left the gallery and were soon out of El Corraln.

"What was the matter?'" asked Manuel.

"Nothing. It's all over now," answered Leandro. "I went in and said to her, nice enough, 'Listen Milagros, is it true that you're going to marry Lechuguino?' 'Yes, it is true. Is it any business of yours?' she says. 'Yes, it is,' I said to her. 'You know that I like you. Is it because he's richer than me?' 'Even if he were poorer than a church-mouse I'd marry him.' 'Bah!' 'You don't believe me?' 'All right.' Finally I got sore and I told her for all I cared she might marry a dog, and that she was a cheap street-walker.... It's all over now. Well, so much the better. Now we know just where we stand. Where shall we go? To Las Injurias again?"

"What for?"

"To see if that Valencia continues to put on airs when I'm around."

They crossed the wired-off surrounding path. Leandro, taking long strides, was very soon in Las Injurias. Manuel could hardly keep up with him.

They entered Blasa's tavern; the same men as on the previous night were playing can near the stove. Of the women, only La Paloma and La Muerte were in. The latter, dead drunk, was asleep on the table. The light fell full upon her face which was swollen with erisypelas and covered with scabs; saliva drooled through the thick lips of her half-opened mouth; her tow-like hair,—grey, filthy, matted,—stuck out in tufts beneath the faded, greenish kerchief that was soiled with scurf; despite the shouts and the disputes of the gamblers she did not so much as blink; only from time to time she would give a prolonged snore, which, at the start was sibilant, but ended in a rasping snort. At her side Paloma, huddled on the floor near Valencia, held a tot of three or four in her arms,—a pale, delicate creature who blinked incessantly,—to whom she was giving whisky from a glass.

A gaunt, weak fellow wearing a small cap with a gilded number and a blue smock, passed moodily up and down before the counter; his arms hung beside his body as if they did not belong to him, and his legs were bent. Whenever it occurred to him, he took a sip from his glass; he wiped his lips with the back of his hand and would resume his languid pacing to and fro. He was the brother of the woman who owned the tavern.

Leandro and Manuel took a seat at the same table where the gamblers were playing. Leandro ordered wine, emptied a deep glass at a single gulp and heaved a few sighs.

"Christ!" muttered Leandro half under his breath. "Never let yourself go wild over a woman. The best of them is as poisonous as a toad."

Then he seemed to calm down. He gazed at the drawings scratched on the top of the table: there were hearts pierced by arrows, the names of women; he drew a knife from his pocket and began to cut letters into the wood.

When he wearied of this he invited one of the gamblers to drink with him.

"Thanks, friend," replied the gambler. "I'm playing."

"All right, leave the game. If you don't want to, nobody'll force you. Doesn't anybody want to drink with me? My treat."

"I'll have one," said a tall, bent fellow with a sickly air, who was called El Pastiri. He arose and came over to Leandro.

Leandro ordered more wine and amused himself by laughing loudly when any one lost and in betting against Valencia.

Pastiri took advantage of the opportunity to empty one glass after the other. He was a sot, a croney of Tabuenca's and likewise dedicated himself to the deception of the unwary with ball-and-number tricks. Manuel knew him from having seen him often on la Ribera de Curtidores. He used to ply his trade in the suburbs, playing at three cards. He would place three cards upon a little table; one of these he would show, then slowly he would change the position of the other two, without touching the card he had shown; he would then place a little stick across the three cards and wager that nobody could pick out the one he had let them see. And so well was the game prepared that the card was never picked.

Pastiri had another trick on the same order, worked with three men from a game of checkers; underneath one of the men he would place a tiny ball of paper or a crumb of bread and then bet that nobody could tell under which of the three ball or crumb was to be found. If, by accident, any one chanced upon the right man, Pastiri would conceal the crumb in his finger-nail as he turned the man up.

That night Pastiri was saturated with alcohol and had lost all power of speech.

Manuel, who had drunk a little too much, was beginning to feel sick and considered how he might manage to make his escape; but by the time he had made up his mind the tavern-keeper's brother was already locking the door.

Before he had quite done so there came in, through the space that was still left open, an under-grown fellow, shaved, dressed in black, with a visored woollen cap, curly hair and the repellant appearance of a hermaphrodite. He greeted Leandro affectionately. He was a lacemaker from Uncle Rilo's house, of dubious repute and called Besugito (sea-bream) because his face suggested a fish; by way of more cruel sobriquet they had christened him the "Barrack hack."

The lacemaker took a sip from a glass, standing, and began to talk in a thick voice; yet it was a feminine voice, unctuous, disagreeable, and he emphasized his words with mimicked wonder, fright, and other mannerisms.

Nobody was bothered by his loquacity. Some fine day when they least expected, he informed them, the entire district of Las Injurias was going to be buried beneath the ruins of the Gas House.

"As far as I'm concerned," he went on, "this entire hollow ought to be filled in with earth. Of course, I'd feel sorry, for I have some good friends in this section."

"Ay! Pass!" said one of the gamblers.

"Yes, I'd be sorry," continued Besuguito, heedless of the interruption. "But the truth is that it would be a small loss, for, as Angelillo, the district watchman says, nobody lives here except outcasts, pickpockets and prostitutes."

"Shut up, you 'fairy!' You barrack hack!" shouted the proprietress. "This district is as good as yours."

"You're right, there," replied Besuguito, "for you ought to see the Portillo de Embajadores and las Peuelas. I tell you. Why, the watchman can't get them to shut their doors at night. He closes them and the neighbours open them again. Because they're almost all denizens of the underworld. And they do give me such frights...."

An uproar greeted the frights of Besuguito, who continued unabashed his meaningless, repetitious chatter, which was adorned with all manner of notions and involutions. Manuel rested an arm upon the table, and with his cheek upon it, he fell asleep.

99

"Hey you! Why aren't you drinking, Pastiri?" asked Leandro. "Do you mean to offend me? Me?"

"No, friend, I simply can't get any more down," answered the card-sharper in his insolent voice, raising his open hand to his throat. Then, in a voice that seemed to come from a broken organ, he shouted:

"Paloma!"

"Who's calling that woman?" demanded Valencia immediately, glaring at the group of gamblers.

"I," answered El Pastiri. "I want Paloma over here."

"Ah!... You? Well, there's nothing doing," declared Valencia.

"I said I want Paloma over here," repeated Pastiri, without looking at the bully.

The latter pretended not to have heard. The card-sharper, provoked by this discourtesy, got up and, slapping Valencia's sleeve with the back of his hand, he repeated his words, dwelling upon every syllable:

"I said that I wanted Paloma, and that these friends of mine want to talk with the lady."

"And I tell you that there's nothing doing," answered the other.

"Those gentlemen want to talk with her."

"All right.... Then let them ask my permission."

Pastiri thrust his face into the bully's, and looking him straight in the eye, croaked:

"Do you realize, Valencia, that you're getting altogether too damned high and mighty?"

"You don't say!" sneered Valencia, calmly continuing his game.

"Do you know that I'm going to let you have a couple with my fist?"

"You don't say!"

Pastiri drew back with drunken awkwardness and began to hunt in the inside pocket of his coat for his knife, amidst the derisive laughter of the bystanders. Then all at once, with a sudden resolve, Leandro jumped to his feet, his face as red as flame; he seized Valencia by the lapel of his coat, gave him a rude tug and sent him smashing against the wall.

The gamblers rushed into the fray; the table was overturned and there was a pandemonium of cries and curses. Manuel awoke with a frightened start. He found himself in the midst of an awful row; most of the gamblers, with the tavern-owner's brother at their head, wanted to throw Leandro out, but the raging youth, backed against the counter, was kicking off anybody that approached him.

"Leave us alone!" shouted Valencia, his lips slavering as he tried to work himself free of the men who were holding him.

"Yes, leave them alone," said one of the gamblers.

"I'll kill the first guy that touches me," warned El Valencia, displaying a long knife with black blades.

"That's the stuff," commented Leandro mockingly. "Let's see who are the red-blooded men."

"Ol!" shouted Pastiri enthusiastically, in his husky voice.

Leandro drew from the inside pocket of his sack-coat a long, narrow knife; the onlookers retreated to the walls so as to leave plenty of room for the duellists. Paloma began to bawl:

"You'll get killed! You'll get killed, I'm telling you!"

"Take that woman away," yelled Valencia in a tragic voice: "Ea!" he added, cleaving the air with his knife. "Now let's see who are the men with guts!"

The two rivals advanced to the centre of the tavern, glaring furiously at each other. The spectators were enthralled by mingled interest and horror.

Valencia was the first to attack; he bent forward as if to seek out where to strike his opponent; he crouched, aimed at the groin and lunged forward upon Leandro; but seeing that Leandro awaited him calmly without retreating, he rapidly recoiled. Then he resumed his false attacks, trying to surprise his adversary with these feints, threatening his stomach yet all the while aiming to stab him in the face; but before the rigid arm of Leandro, who seemed to be sparing every motion until he should strike a sure blow, the bully grew disconcerted and once again drew back. Then Leandro advanced. The youth came on with such sangfroid that he struck terror into his opponent's heart; his face bespoke his determination to transfix Valencia. An oppressive silence weighed upon the tavern; only the sounds of Paloma's convulsive sobs were heard from the adjoining room.

Valencia, divining Leandro's resolve, grew so pale that his face turned a sickly blue, his eyes distended and his teeth began to chatter. At Leandro's first lunge he retreated, but remained on guard; then his fear overcame him and abandoning all thought of attack he took to flight, knocking over the chairs. Leandro, blind, smiling cruelly, gave implacable pursuit.

It was a sad, painful sight; all the partizans of the bully began to eye him with scorn.

"Now, you yellow-liver, you show the white feather!" shouted Pastiri. "You're flitting about like a grasshopper. Off with you, my boy! You're in for it! If you don't get out right away you'll be feeling a palm's length of steel in your ribs!"

One of Leandro's thrusts ripped the bully's jacket.

The thug, now possessed of the wildest panic, dashed behind the counter; his popping eyes reflected mad terror.

Leandro, insolently scornful, stood rigidly in the middle of the tavern; pulling the springs of his knife, he closed it. A murmur of admiration arose from the spectators.

Valencia uttered a cry of pain, as if he had been wounded; his honour, his repute as a bold man, had suffered a downfall. Desperately he made his way to the door of the back room, and looked at the panting proprietress. She must have understood him, for she passed him a key and Valencia sneaked out. But soon the door of the back room opened and the bully stood there anew; brandishing his long knife by the point he threw it furiously at Leandro's face. The weapon whizzed through the air like a terrible arrow and pierced the wall, where it stuck, quivering.

At once Leandro sprang up, but Valencia had disappeared. Then, having recovered from the surprise, the youth calmly dislodged the knife, closed it and handed it to the tavern-keeper.

"When a fellow don't know how to use these things," he said, petulantly, "he ought to keep away from them. Tell that gentleman so when you next see him."

The proprietress answered with a grunt, and Leandro sat down to receive general congratulations upon his courage and his coolness; everybody wanted to treat him.

"This Valencia was beginning to make too much trouble, anyway," said one of them. "Did as he pleased every night and he got away with it because it was Valencia; but he was getting too darned fresh."

"That's what," replied another of the players, a grim old jailbird who had escaped from the Ceuta penitentiary and who looked just like a fox. "When a guy has the nerve, he rakes in all the dough," and he made a gesture of scooping up all the coins on the table in his fingers—"and he skips."

"But this Valencia is a coward," said Pastiri in his thick voice. "A big mouth with a bark worse than his bite and not worth a slap."

"He was on his guard right away. In case of accident!" replied Besuguito in his queer voice, imitating the posture of one who is about to attack with a knife.

"I tell you," exclaimed El Pastiri, "he's a booby, and he's scared so stiff he can't stand."

"Yes, but he answered every thrust, just the same," added the lace-maker.

"Yah! Did you see him?"

"Certainly."

"Bah, you must be soused to the gills!"

"You only wish you were as sober as I. Bah!"

"What? You're so full you can't talk!"

"Go on; shut up. You're so drunk you can't stand; I tell you, if you run afoul of this guy"—and Besuguito pointed to Leandro—"you're in for a bad time."

"Hell, no!"

"That's my opinion, anyhow."

"You don't have any opinion here, or anything like it," exclaimed Leandro. "You're going to clear out and shut up. Valencia's liver is whiter than paper; it's as Pastiri says. Brave enough when it comes to exploiting boobs like you and the other tramps and low lives,... but when he bucks up against a chap that's all there, hey? Bah! He's a white-livered wretch, that's what."

"True," assented all.

"And maybe we won't let him hear a few things," said the escaped convict, "if he has the nerve to return here for his share of the winnings."

"I should say!" exclaimed Pastiri.

"Very well, gentlemen, it's my treat now," said Leandro, "for I've got the money and I happen to feel like it." He fished out a couple of coins from his pocket and slapped them down on the table. "Lady, let's have something to drink."

"Right away."

"Manuel! Manuel!" shouted Leandro several times. "Where in thunder has that kid disappeared?"

Manuel, following the example of the bully, had made his escape by the back door.

CHAPTER IX

An Unlikely Tale—Manuel's Sisters—Life's Baffling Problems.

It was already the beginning of autumn; Leandro, on the advice of Seor Ignacio, was living with his aunt on Aguila street; Milagros continued keeping company with Lechuguino. Manuel gave up going with Vidal and Bizco on their skirmishes and joined the company of Rebolledo and the two Aristas.

The elder, Aristn, entertained him and frightened him out of his wits with lugubrious tales of cemeteries and ghosts; the little Aristas continued his gymnastic exercises; he had constructed a springboard by placing a plank upon a heap of sand and there he practised his death-defying leaps.

One day Alonso, Tabuenca's aid, appeared in the Corraln accompanied by a woman and a little girl.

The woman seemed old and weary; the tot was long and thin and pale. Don Alonso found them a place in a dingy corner of the small patio.

They brought with them a small bundle of clothes, a dirty poodle with a very intelligent look, and a monkey tied to a chain; in a short while they had to sell the monkey to some gipsies that lived in the Quinta de Goya.

Don Alonso called Manuel and said to him:

"Run off and hunt up Don Roberto, and tell him that there's a woman here named Rosa, and that she is or has been a circus acrobat; she must be the one he's looking for."

At once Manuel went off to the house; Roberto had left the place and Manuel did not know his whereabouts.

Don Alonso carne frequently to the Corraln and conversed with the mother and the girl. On the window-sill of their tiny home the mother and the daughter had a little box with a sprig of mint planted in it; although they watered it every morning, it scarcely grew, for there was no sun. One day the woman and child disappeared together with their pretty poodle; they left nothing in their quarters except a worn-out, broken tambourine.

Don Alonso got into the habit of visiting the Corraln; he would exchange a few words with Rebolledo, he of the modernist barber-shop who chattered away, and would witness the gymnastic prowess of Aristas. One afternoon the boy's mother asked the former Snake-Man whether the child showed any real aptitude.

Don Alonso grew serious and subjected the boy's performance to a searching examination, so that he could form an estimate of the youngster's abilities and give him a little useful advice.

It was really curious to see the former circus-player give his orders; he went through them with august seriousness.

"One, two, three.... Hop-la!... Once more, now. At position. The knees near the head ... nails down ... One, two ... one, two.... Hop-la!"

Don Alonso was not at all displeased with little Aristas' showing, but he emphasized the unavoidable necessity of continual hard practise.

"Whoever wants something has to pay the price, my little fellow," he said. "And the profession of gymnast isn't within everybody's reach."

To the mother he confided that her son might some day be a fine circus artist.

Then Don Alonso, finding himself before a numerous public, would begin to talk volubly of the United States, of Mexico, and the South American republics.

"Why don't you tell us stories of the countries you've been to?" asked Perico Rebolledo.

"No, not now; I have to go out with the *Infiel* Tower."

"Ah! Go on, tell us," they would all implore.

Don Alonso pretended to be importuned by the request; but when he got going, he spun one yarn after the other in such numbers that they almost had to beg him to stop.

"And didn't you ever see in those countries men who had been killed by lions?" asked Aristn.

"No."

"Then there aren't any lions?"

"Lions in cages ... yes, a lot."

"But I mean at liberty, in the fields."

"In the fields? No."

106

Don Alonso seemed rather provoked to make these confessions.

"No other wild beasts, either?"

"There are no longer any wild beasts in the civilized countries," said the barber.

"Why, see here, there certainly are wild beasts over there," and Don Alonso, wrinkling his features into a jesting grimace, winked slily at Rebolledo. "Once a terrible thing happened to me; we were sailing by an island when we heard cannon shots. It was the garrison firing off a salvo."

"But what are you laughing at?" asked Aristn.

"Nervousness.... Well, as I was saying, I went up to the captain of the ship and asked his permission to let me land on the island. 'Very well,' he said to me, 'take the Golondrina, if you wish,'—Golondrina was the name of the canoe; 'but you must be back within a couple of hours.'

"I set off in my boat and hala! hala! ... I reached the island, which was thickly planted with plane-trees and cocoanut-trees, and I disembarked on the beach into which the Golondrina had thrust its prow."

Here Don Alonso's features were convulsed with the impossibility of restraining his laughter; he shot a glance at the barber, accompanied by a confidential wink.

"I land," he continued, "then I start running, and soon, paf! ... in the face; a huge mosquito, and then, paf! ... another mosquito, until I was surrounded by a swarm of the animals, each one as large as a bat. With a scarred face I begin to run for the beach so as to escape in my canoe, when I catch sight of a lobster right next to the Golondrina; but what a lobster I He must have been as big as a bear; he was black, and shiny, and went chug, chug, chug, like an automobile. No sooner did the creature set eyes on me than he began to rush upon me with loud outcries; I ran for a cocoanut tree, and one, two, three, I shinnied right up the trunk to the top. The lobster approaches the tree, stops meditatively, and decides to shinny up after me,— which he did."

"An awful situation," commented the barber.

"Just imagine," replied Don Alonso, blinking. "I only had a little stick in my hands, and I defended myself against the lobster by hitting him in the knuckles; but he, roaring with rage, and eyes shining, continued climbing. I couldn't get any farther, and I was thinking of coming down; but as I made a movement, biff!... The son of a sea-cook grabs me with one of his many legs by the coat and remains there hanging from me. The cussed critter was as heavy as lead; he was already reaching up after me with another claw when I remembered that I had in my vest pocket a toothpick that I had bought in Chicago, and that it had a knife attachment; I opened this, and in a moment slashed off the tail of my coat, and cataplun! ... down from a height of at least forty metres the lobster fell to the ground. I can't understand how he wasn't killed. There he began to cry and howl, and go round and round the cocoanut tree in which I was, glaring at me with his terrible eyes. Whereupon I—for being a gymnast had to come in handy to a fellow,—began to leap from one cocoanut tree to the next and from one plane-tree to the other, while the lobster kept following me, howling away with the tail of my coat in his teeth.

"Reaching near the beach I find that the tide has gone out and that the Golondrina is more than fifty metres above the waves. 'I'll wait,' I said to myself. But at this moment I see, thrusting its head out from the tree-top that I was then on, a serpent; I seize a branch, swing up and back for a while so that I can land as far as possible from the lobster, when the damned branch breaks on me and I lose my support."

"And what did you do then?" asked the barber.

"I took two somersaults in the air at a hazard."

"That was a useful precaution."

"Certainly I thought I was lost. On the contrary, I was saved."

"But how?" asked El Aristn.

"Very simple. For as I fell, with the branch in my hand, I landed plump on the lobster, and as I came down with such a high velocity, I pierced him right through with the branch and left him nailed to the beach. The animal roared like a bull; I jumped into the Golondrina and made my escape. But my vessel had sailed away. I began to row, but there wasn't a sail in sight. 'I'm lost,' says I to myself. But thanks to the lobster, I was rescued...."

"The lobster?" asked everybody in amazement.

"Yes sirree; a steamboat that was on its course many miles off, on hearing the lobster's wails thought that this might be the signal of some shipwrecked crew; it drew near the island, picked me up, and in a few days I was back with my company."

As he finished his tale Don Alonso made a most expressive grimace, and left with his *Infiel* Tower for the street. Aristas, Rebolledo and Manuel applauded the old circus man's stories, and the apprentice gymnast felt more determined than ever to continue practicing upon the trapeze and the springboard, so that some day he might behold those distant lands of which Don Alonso spoke.

A few weeks later there occurred one of the events that left upon Manuel the deepest impression of his entire career. It was Sunday; the boy went to his mother's place, and helped her, as usual, to wash the dishes. Then came Petra's daughters, and they

108

spent the whole afternoon quarrelling over a skirt or a petticoat that the younger had bought with the elder sister's money.

Manuel, bored by the chatter, invented some excuse and left the house.

The rain was coming down in bucketfuls; Manuel reached the Puerta del Sol, entered the caf de Levante and sat down near the window. The people outside, dressed in their Sunday clothes, scampered by to places of refuge in the wide doorways of the big square; the coaches rumbled hurriedly on amidst the downpour; umbrellas came and went and their black tops, glistening with rain, collided and intertwined like a shoal of tortoises. Presently it cleared up and Manuel left the caf; it was still too early to return to the house; he crossed the Plaza de Oriente and stopped on the Viaduct, watching from that point the people strolling along Segovia street.

In the sky, which was becoming serene, floated a few dark clouds with silver linings, resembling mountains capped with snow; blown by the wind, they scurried along with outspread wings; the bright sun illumined the fields with its golden rays; resplendent in the clouds, it reddened them like live coals; a few cloudlets scudded through space, white flakes of foam. The hillocks and dales of the Madrilenian suburbs were not yet mottled with green grass; the trees of the Campo del Moro stood out reddish, skeleton-like, amidst the foliage of the evergreens; dark rolls of vapour rose along the ground, soon to be swept away by the wind. As the clouds passed by overhead, the plain changed hue; successively it graded from purple into leaden-grey, yellow, copper; the Extremadura cart-road, with the rows of grey, dirty houses on each side, traced a broken line. This severe, melancholy landscape of the Madrilenian suburbs, with their bleak, cold gloominess, penetrated into Manuel's soul.

He left the Viaduct balcony, sauntered through several narrow lanes, until he reached Toledo Street, walked down the Ronda and turned in toward his house. He was getting near the Paseo de las Acacias when he overheard two old women talking about a crime that had just been committed at the corner of Amparo Street.

"And just as they were about to catch him, he killed himself," one of them was saying.

Out of curiosity Manuel hastened his step, and approached a group that was discussing the event at the entrance to the Corraln.

"Where did this fellow come from that killed himself?" asked Manuel of Aristas.

"Why! It was Leandro!"

"Leandro!"

"Yes, Leandro, who killed Milagros and then killed himself."

"But ... is this really so?"

"Yes, man. Just a moment ago,"

"Here? In the house?"

"On this very spot."

Manuel, quaking with fear, ran up the stairs to the gallery. The floor was still stained with the pool of blood. Seor Zurro, the only witness to the drama, was telling the story to a group of neighbours.

"I was here, reading the paper," said the old-clothes man, "and Milagros and her mother were talking to Lechuguino. The engaged couple were enjoying themselves, when up comes Leandro to the gallery; he was about to open the door to his rooms when, before he went in, he suddenly turned to Milagros. 'Is that your sweetheart?' he said to her. It seemed to me that he was as pale as a corpse. 'Yes,' she answered. 'All right. Then I've come here to end things once and for all,' he shouted. 'Which of the two do you prefer, him or me?' 'Him,' shrieks Milagros. 'Then it's all up,' cried Leandro in a hoarse voice. 'I'm going to kill you.' After that I can't recall anything clearly; it was all as swift as a thunderbolt; when I ran over to them, the girl was gushing blood from her mouth; the proof-reader's wife was screaming and Leandro was chasing Lechuguino with his knife opened."

"I saw him leave the house," added an old woman. "He was waving his blood-stained knife in the air; my husband tried to stop him; but he backed like a bull, lunged for him and came near killing him."

"And where are my uncle and aunt?" asked Manuel.

"Over at the Emergency Hospital. They followed the stretcher."

Manuel went down into the patio.

"Where are you going?" asked Aristn.

"To the Emergency Hospital."

"I'll go along with you."

The two boys were joined by a machine shop apprentice who lived in the Corrala.

"I saw him kill himself," said the apprentice. "We were all running after him, hollering, 'Catch him! Stop him!' when two guards appeared on Amparo Street, drew their swords and blocked his way. Then Leandro bounded back, made his way

110

through the people and landed here again; he was going to escape through the Paseo de las Acacias when he stumbled against La Muerte, who began to call him names. Leandro stopped, looked in every direction; nobody dared to get near him; his eyes were blazing. Suddenly he jabbed the knife into his left side I don't know how many times. When one of the guards seized him by the arm he collapsed like an empty sack."

The commentary of Aristn and the apprentice proved endless; the boys arrived at the Emergency Hospital and were told that the corpses, those of Milagros and Leandro, had been taken to the Morgue. The three gamins walked down to the Canal, to the little house near the river's edge, which Manuel and the urchins of his gang had so often visited, trying to peep into the windows. A knot of people had gathered about the door.

"Let's have a look," said Aristn.

There was a window, wide open, and they peered in. Stretched upon a marble slab lay Leandro; his face was the color of wax, and his features bore an expression of proud defiance. At his side Seora Leandro stood wailing and vociferating; Seor Ignacio, with his son's hand clasped in his own, was weeping silently. At another table a group surrounded Milagros' corpse. The man in charge of the morgue ordered them all out. As the proofreader and Seor Ignacio met at the entrance they exchanged looks and then averted their glance; the two mothers, on the other hand, glared at each other in terrible hatred.

Seor Ignacio arranged that they should not sleep at the Corraln but in Aguila Street. In that place, at the home of Seora Jacoba, there was a horrible confusion of weeping and cursing. The three women blamed Milagros for everything; she was a common strumpet, an evil woman, a selfish, wretched ingrate.

One of the neighbours of the Corrala indicated a strange detail: when the public doctor came to examine Milagros and remove her corset so that he might determine the wound, he found a tiny medallion containing a portrait of Leandro.

"Whose picture is this?" he is reported to have asked.

"The fellow who killed her," they answered. This was exceedingly strange, and it fascinated Manuel; many a time he had thought that Milagros really loved Leandro; this fairly confirmed his conjectures.

During all that night Seor Ignacio, seated on a chair, wept without cease; Vidal was scared through and through, as was Manuel. The presence of death, seen so near, had terrorized the two boys.

And while inside the house everybody was crying, in the streets the little girls were dancing around in a ring. And this contrast of anguish and serenity, of grief and calm, imparted to Manuel a confused sense of life. It must, he thought, be something exceedingly sad, and something weirdly inscrutable.

PART THREE

CHAPTER I

Uncle Patas' Domestic Drama—The Bakery—Karl the Baker—The Society of the Three.

The death of his son made such a deep impression upon Seor Ignacio that he fell ill. He gave up working in the shop and as he showed no improvement after two or three weeks, Leandra said to Manuel:

"See here: better be off to your mother's place, for I can't keep you here."

Manuel returned to the lodging-house and Petra, through the intercession of the landlady, procured her son a job as errand-boy at a bread and vegetable stand situated upon the Plaza del Carmen.

Manuel was here more oppressed than at Seor Ignacio's. Uncle Patas, the proprietor, a heavy, burly Galician, instructed the youth in his duties.

He was to get up at daybreak, open the store, untie the bundles of greens that were brought by a boy from the Plaza de la Cebada and receive the bread that was left by the delivery-men. Then he was to sweep the place and wait for Uncle Patas, his wife or sister-in-law to awake. As soon as one of these came in Manuel would leave his place behind the counter and, balancing a little basket upon his head, would start off on his route delivering bread to the customers of the vicinity. This going and returning would take all the morning. In the afternoon the work was harder: Manuel would have to stand quietly behind the counter in utter boredom, under the surveillance of the proprietor's wife and his sister-in-law.

Accustomed to his daily strolls through the Rondas, Manuel was rendered desperate by this immobility.

Uncle Patas' store, a tiny, ill-smelling hole, was papered in yellow with green borders; the paper was coming off from sheer old age. A wooden counter, a few dirty shelves, an oil lamp hanging from the ceiling and two benches comprised the fixtures.

The back room, which was reached by a door at the rear, was a compartment with no more light than could filter in through a transom that opened upon the vestibule. This was the dining-room and led to the kitchen, which in turn gave access to a narrow, very filthy patio with a fountain. At the other side of the patio were the bedrooms of Uncle Patas, his wife and his sister-in-law.

Manuel's sleeping quarters were a straw-bed and a couple of old cloaks behind the counter. Here, especially at night, it reeked of rotten cabbage: but what bothered Manuel even more was the getting up at dawn, when the watchman struck two or three blows with his pike upon the door of the store.

They sold something in the shop,—enough to live on and no more. In this hovel Uncle Patas had saved up a fortune cntimo by cntimo.

Uncle Patas' history was really interesting. Manuel had learned it from the gossip of the men who delivered the bread and from the boys in the other stores.

Uncle Patas had come to Madrid from a hamlet of Lugo, at the age of fifteen, in search of a living. Within twenty years, by dint of unbelievable economies, he had hoarded up from his wages in a bakery some three or four thousand pesetas, and with this capital he established a little grocery. His wife stood behind the counter while he continued to work in the bakery and hoard his earnings. When his son grew up he assigned to the boy the running of a tavern and then of a pawnbroker-shop. It was during this prosperous epoch that Uncle Patas' wife died, and the man, now a widower, wishing to taste the sweets of life, which had thus far proved so fruitless, married again despite his fifty-odd years; the bride, a lass that came from his own province, was only twenty and her sole object in marrying was to change from servant to mistress. All of Uncle Patas' friends tried to convince him that it was a monstrosity for a man of his years to wed, and such a young girl at that; but he persisted in his notions and married.

Within two months after the marriage the son had come to an understanding with his step-mother, and shortly after this the elderly husband made the discovery. One day he played the spy and saw his son and his wife leave an assignation house in Santa Margarita Street. Perhaps the man intended to take harsh steps, to speak a few unvarnished words to the couple; but as he was soft and peaceful by nature, and did not wish to disturb his business, he let the time go by and grew little by little accustomed to his position. Somewhat later, Uncle Patas' wife brought from her town a sister of hers, and when she arrived, between the wife and the son she was forced upon the old man, who concluded by taking up with his sister-in-law. Since that time the four had lived in unbroken harmony. They understood one another most admirably.

Manuel was not in the least astonished by this state of affairs; he was cured of fear, for at La Corrala there was more than one matrimonial combination of the sort. What did make him indignant was the stinginess of Uncle Patas and his people.

All the scrupulousness which Uncle Patas' wife did not feel in other matters she reserved, no doubt, for the accounts. Herself accustomed to pilfer, she knew to the least detail every trick of the servants, and not a cntimo escaped her; she always thought she was being robbed. Such was her spirit of economy that at home they ate stale bread, thus confirming the popular saying, "in the house of the smith, a wooden knife."

The sister-in-law, an uncouth peasant with a stubby nose, carroty cheeks, abundant breasts and hips, could give lessons in avarice to her sister, while in the matter of immodesty and undignified comportment she outdistanced her. She would go about the store with her bosom exposed and there wasn't a delivery-man who missed a chance to pinch her.

"What a fatty you are! Oh!" they would all exclaim.

And it was as if all this frequently fingered fat didn't belong to her, for she raised no protest. Should any one, however, try to get the best of her on the price of a roll, she would turn into a wild beast.

On Sunday afternoons Uncle Patas, his wife and his sister-in-law were in the habit of playing *mus* on a little table in the middle of the road; they never dared to leave the store alone.

After Manuel had been here for three months, Petra came to see Uncle Patas and asked him to give her boy a regular wage. Uncle Patas burst into laughter; the request struck him as the very height of absurdity and he answered No, that it was impossible, that the boy didn't even earn the bread he ate.

Then Petra sought out another place for Manuel and brought him to a bakery on Horno de la Mata Street where he was to learn the trade.

As the beginning of his apprenticeship he was assigned to the furnace as assistant to the man who removed the loaves from the oven. The work was beyond his strength. He had to get up at eleven in the night and commence by scraping the iron pans in which the smaller loaves were baked; after they were cleaned he would go over them with a brush dipped in melted butter; this accomplished he would help his superior remove the live coals from the oven with an iron instrument; then, while the baker baked the bread he would lift very heavy boards laden with rolls and carry them to the kneading-trough at the mouth of the furnace; when the baker placed the rolls inside Manuel would take the board back to the kneading-trough. As the bread came out of the oven he would moisten it with a brush dipped in water so as to make the crust shiny. At eleven in the morning the work was over, and during the intervals of idleness Manuel and the workmen would sleep.

This life was horribly hard.

The bakery occupied a dark cellar, as gloomy as it was dirty. It was below the level of the street and had two windows the panes of which were so covered with dust and spiders' webs that only a murky, yellowish light filtered through. They worked at all hours by gas.

The bakery was entered by a door that opened upon an ample patio, in which was a shed of pierced zinc; this protected from the rain, or tried to protect, at least, the loads of furze branch and the piles of wood that were heaped up there.

116

From this patio a low door gave access to a long, but narrow and damp, corridor that was everywhere black; only at the extreme end there was a square of light that entered through a high window with a few cracked, filthy panes,—a gloomy illumination.

When the eyes grew accustomed to the surrounding gloom they could make out on the wall some delivery-baskets, bakers' peels, smocks, caps and shoes hanging from nails, and on the ceiling thick, silvery cobwebs covered with dust.

Half way along the corridor were a couple of doors opposite each other; one led to the furnace, the other to the kneading room.

The furnace room was spacious, and the walls filmed with soot, so that the place was as black as a camera obscura; a gas-jet burned in that cavern, illuminating almost nothing. Before the mouth of the furnace, against an iron shed, were placed the shovels; above, on the ceiling, could be made out some large pipes that crossed each other.

The kneading room, less dark than the furnace room, was even more somber. A pallid light shone in through the two windows that looked into the patio, their panes encrusted with flour dust. There were always some ten or twelve men in shirt-sleeves, brandishing their arms desperately over the troughs, and in the back of the room a she-mule slowly turned the kneading machine.

Life in the bakery was disagreeable and hard; the work was enervating and the pay small: seven reales per day. Manuel, unaccustomed to the heat of the furnace, turned dizzy; besides, when he moistened the loaves fresh from the oven he would burn his fingers and it disgusted him to see his hands begrimed with grease and soot.

He was also unlucky enough to have his bed placed in the kneaders' room, beside that of an old workman of the shop who suffered from chronic catarrh, as a result of having breathed so much flour into his lungs; this fellow kept hawking away at all hours.

From sheer disgust Manuel found it impossible to sleep here, so he went to the furnace kitchen and threw himself down upon the floor. He was forever weary; but despite this, he worked automatically.

Then nobody paid any attention to him; the other bakers, a gang of pretty rough Galicians, treated him as if he were a mule; none of them even took the trouble to learn his name, and some addressed him, "Hey, you, Choto!" while others cried "Hello, Barriga!" When they spoke of him they referred to him as "the ragamuffin from Madrid" or simply, "ragamuffin." He answered to whatever names and sobriquets they gave him.

At first the most hateful of all these men, to Manuel, was the head baker, who ordered him about in a despotic manner and grew angry if things weren't done in a trice. This baker was a German named Karl Schneider who had come to Spain as a vagrant, in evasion of military service. He was about twenty-four or twenty-five, with limpid eyes, and hair and moustache that were so fair as almost to be white.

A timid, phlegmatic fellow, he was frightened by everything and found all things difficult. His strong impressions were manifested neither in his motions nor his words, but in a sudden flush, which coloured his cheeks and his forehead, and which would soon disappear and leave an intense pallor.

Karl expressed himself very well in Spanish, but in a rare manner; he knew a string of proverbs and phrases which he entangled inextricably; this lent a quaint character to his conversation.

Manuel soon discovered that the German, despite his abruptness, was a fine fellow, very innocent, very sentimental and of paradisiacal simplicity.

After a month's work in the bakery Manuel had come to consider Karl as his only friend; they treated each other as boon companions and addressed each other in familiar terms; and if the baker often helped his assistant in any task that required strength, he would in his turn, on occasion, ask the boy's opinion and consult him regarding sentimental complications and punctilios, which fascinated the German and which Manuel settled with his natural perspicacity and the instincts of a wandering child who has been convinced that all life's motives are egotistical and base. This equality between master and apprentice disappeared the moment Karl took up his position at the mouth of the furnace. At such times Manuel had to obey the German without cavil or delay.

Karl's one vice was drunkenness; he was forever thirsty; whenever he slaked this thirst with wine and beer everything went well; he led a methodical life and would spend his free hours on the Pinza, de Oriente or in the Moncloa, reading the two volumes that comprised his library: one, *Lost Illusions*, by Balzac and the other, a collection of German poems.

These two books, constantly read, commented upon and annotated by him, filled his head with fancies and dreams. Between the bitter, despairing, yet fundamentally romantic ratiocinations of Balzac, and the idealities of Goethe and Heine, the poor baker dwelt in the most unreal of worlds. Often Karl would explain to Manuel the conflicts between the persons of his favourite novel, and would ask how he would act under similar circumstances. Manuel would usually hit upon so logical, so natural, so little romantic a solution that the German would stand perplexed and fascinated before the boy's clearness of judgment; but soon, considering the selfsame theme anew, he would see that such a solution would prove valueless to his sublimated personages, for the very conflict of the novel would never have come about amidst folk of common thoughts.

118

There came stretches of ten or twelve days when the German needed more powerful stimulants than wine and literature, and he would get drunk on whisky, drinking down half a flask as if it were so much water.

According to what he told Manuel, he was overwhelmed by an avalanche of sadness; everything looked black and repulsive to his eyes, he felt feverish and the one remedy for this melancholy was alcohol.

When he entered the tavern his heart was heavy and his head dull with a surfeit of ugly notions, but as he drank he felt his heart grow lighter and his breath come easier, while his head began to dance with merry thoughts. When he left the tavern, however hard he tried, it was impossible for him to preserve his dignity; laughter would flicker upon his lips. Then songs of his native land would throng to his memory and he would sing them aloud, beating time to them as he walked on. As long as he went through the central thoroughfares he would walk straight; no sooner did he reach the back streets, the deserted avenues, than he would abandon himself to the pleasure of stumbling along and staggering, with a bump here and a thump there. During these moods everything seemed great and beautiful and superb to the German; the sentimentalism of his race would overflow and he would begin to recite verses and weep, and of whatever acquaintances he met on the street he would beg forgiveness for his imaginary offence, asking anxiously whether he still continued to enjoy their estimation and offering his friendship.

However drunk he might be, he never forgot his duty and when the hour for starting the night's baking arrived he would stagger off to the bakery; the moment he took up his position before the mouth of the furnace his intoxication evaporated and he set to work as soberly as ever, himself laughing at his extravagances.

The German possessed remarkable organic powers and unheard-of resistance; Manuel had to sleep during all his free time, and even at that never rose from his bed completely rested. For the two months that he spent in the bakery Manuel lived like an automaton. Work at the furnace had so shifted about his hours of sleep that the days seemed to him nights and the nights, days.

One day Manuel fell ill and all the strength that had been sustaining him abandoned him suddenly; he gave up his job, took his two-week's pay and without knowing how, fairly dragging himself thither, made his way to the lodging-house.

Petra, finding him in this condition, made him go to bed, and Manuel lay for nearly two weeks in the delirium of a very high fever. On getting out it seemed that he had grown; he was much emaciated, and felt in his whole body a great lassitude and languor and such a keen sensitivity that any word the least mite too harsh would affect him to the point of tears.

When he was able to go out into the street again, he bought, at Petra's suggestion, a gold-plated brooch which he presented to Doa Casiana; she was so pleased with the gift that she told her servant the boy might remain in the house until he was completely recovered.

Those days were among the most pleasant that Manuel ever spent in his whole life; the one thing that bothered him was hunger.

The weather was superb and in the mornings Manuel would go strolling along the Retiro. The journalist whom they called Superman employed Manuel in copying his notes and articles, and as compensation, no doubt, let him take novels by Paul de Kock and Pigault-Lebrun, some of them highly spiced, as for example *Nuns and Corsairs* and *That Rascal Gustave*.

The love theories of these two writers convinced Manuel so well that he tried to put them into practise with the landlady's niece. During the previous two years she had developed so fully that she was already a woman.

One night, during the early hour after supper, either through the influence of the spring season or in obedience to the theories of the author of *Nuns and Corsairs*, Manuel persuaded the landlady's girl of the advantages of a very private consultation, and a neighbour saw the two of them depart together upstairs and enter the garret.

As they were about to shut themselves in, the neighbour surprised them and brought them, deeply contrite, into the presence of Doa Casiana. The thrashing that the landlady administered to her niece deprived the girl of all desire for new adventures and the aunt of any strength to administer another to Manuel.

"Out into the street with you!" she bawled at him, seizing him by the arm and sinking her nails into his flesh. "And make sure that I never see you here again, for I'll brain you!"

Manuel, stricken with shame and confusion, wished nothing better at that moment than a chance to escape, and he dashed into the street as fast as he could get there, like a beaten cur. The night was cool and inviting. As he didn't have a cntimo, he soon wearied of sauntering about; he called at the bakery, asked for Karl the baker, they opened the place to him and he stretched himself out on one of the beds. At dawn he was awakened by the voice of one of the bakers, who was shouting:

"Hey, you! Loafer! Clear out!"

Manuel got up and went out into the street. He strolled along toward the Viaduct, to his favourite spot, to survey the landscape and Segovia street.

It was a glorious spring morning. In the grove near the Campo del Moro some soldiers were drilling to the sound of bugle and drums; from a stone chimney on the Ronda de Segovia puffs of dark smoke issued forth to stain the clear, diaphanous

120

sky; in the laundries on the banks of the Manzanares the clothes hung out to dry shone with a white refulgence.

Manuel slowly crossed the Viaduct, reached Las Vistillas and watched some rag-dealers sorting out their materials after emptying the contents of their sacks upon the ground. He sat down for a while in the sun. With his eyes narrowed to a slit he could make out the arches of the Almudena church just above a wall; beyond rose the Royal Palace, a glittering white, the sandy clearings of the Principe Po with its long red barracks, and the row of houses on the Paseo de Rosales, their panes aglow with the sunlight.

Toward the Casa de Campo several brown, bare knolls stood out, topped by two or three pines that looked as if they had been cut out and pasted upon the blue atmosphere.

From Las Vistillas Manuel walked down to the Ronda de Segovia. As he sauntered along Aguila Street he noticed that Seor Ignacio's place was still closed. Manuel went into the house and asked in the patio for Salom.

"She must be at work in the house," they told him.

He climbed up the stairway and knocked at the door; from within came the hum of a sewing-machine.

Salom opened the door and Manuel entered. The seamstress was as pretty as ever, and, as ever, working. Her two boys had not yet entered colegio. Salom told Manuel that Seor Ignacio had been in hospital and that he was now looking around for some money with which to pay off his debts and continue his business. Leandra at that moment was down by the river, Seor Jacoba at her post, and Vidal loafing around with no desire to work. He simply couldn't be kept away from the company of a certain cross-eyed wretch who was worse than disease itself, and had become a tramp. The two of them were always seen with bad women in the stands and lunch-rooms of the Andaluca road.

Manuel told her of his experiences as a baker and how he had fallen ill; what he did not relate however, was the tale of his dismissal from the house where his mother was employed.

"That's no kind of job for you. You ought to learn some trade that requires less strength," was Salom's advice.

Manuel spent the whole morning chatting with the seamstress; she invited him to a bite and he accepted with pleasure.

In the afternoon Manuel left Salom's house with the thought that if he were a few years older and had a decent, paying position, he would marry her, even if he found himself compelled to get the tough who went with her out of the way with a knife.

Once again upon the Ronda, the first thought that came to Manuel was that he ought not to go to the Toledo Bridge, nor be in any greater hurry to reach the Andaluca road, for it was very easy to happen upon Vidal or Bizco there. He pondered the thought deeply, and yet, despite this, he took the direction of the bridge, glanced into the sands, and failing to find his friends there continued along the Canal, crossed the Manzanares by one of the laundry bridges and came out on Andaluca road. In a lunch-room that sheltered a few tables beneath its roof were Vidal and Bizco in company of a group of idlers playing can.

"Hey, you, Vidal!" shouted Manuel.

"The deuce! Is it you?" exclaimed his cousin.

"As you see...."

"And what are you doing?"

"Nothing. And you?"

"Whatever comes our way."

Manuel watched them play can. After they had finished a hand, Vidal said:

"What do you say to a walk?"

"Come on."

"Are you coming, Bizco?"

"Yes."

The three set out along the Andaluca road.

Vidal and Bizco led a thieves' existence, stealing here a horse blanket, there the electric bulbs of a staircase or telephone wires; whatever turned up. They did not venture to operate in the heart of Madrid as they were not yet, in their opinion, sufficiently expert.

Only a few days before, told Vidal, they had, between them, robbed a fellow of a she-goat, on the banks of the Manzanares near the Toledo bridge. Vidal had entertained the chap at the game of tossing coins while Bizco had seized the goat and pulled her up the slope of the pines to Las Yeseras, afterward taking her to Las Injurias. Then Vidal, indicating the opposite direction to their dupe, had shouted: "Run, run, there goes your goat." And as the youth trotted off in the direction indicated, Vidal escaped to Las Injurias, joining Bizco and his sweetheart. They were still dining on the goat's meat.

"That's what you ought to do," suggested Vidal. "Come with us. This is the life of a lord! Why, listen here. The other day Juan el Burra and El Arenero came upon a dead hog on the road to Las Yeseras. A swineherd was on his way with a herd of them to the slaughter-house, when they found out that the animal had died; the fellow left it there, and Juan el Burra and El Arenero dragged it to their house, quartered it, and we friends of his have been eating hog for more than a week. I tell you, it's a lord's life!"

According to what Vidal said, all the thieves knew each other, even to the most distant sections of the city. Their life was outside the pale of society and an admirable one, indeed; today they were to meet at the Four Roads, in three or four days at the Vallecas Bridge or at La Guindelara; they helped each other.

Their radius of activities was a zone bounded by the extreme of the Casa del Campo, where the inn of Agapito and the Alcorcn restaurants were, as far as Los Carabancheles; from here, the banks of the Abronigal, La Elipa, El Este, Las Ventas and La Conceptin as far as La Prosperidad; then Tetun as far as the Puerta de Hierro. In summer they slept in yards and sheds of the suburbs.

The thieves of the city's centre were a better-dressed, more aristocratic lot; each of these had his woman, whose earnings he managed and who took good care of him. The outcasts of the heart of the city were a distinct class with other gradations.

There were times when Bizco and Vidal had gone through intense want, existing upon cats and rats and seeking shelter in the caves upon San Blas hill, of Madrid Moderno, and in the Eastern Cemetery. But by this time the pair knew their business.

"And work? Nothing?" asked Manuel.

"Work! ... Let the cat work," scoffed Vidal.

They didn't work, stuttered Bizco; who was going to get fresh with him while he had his trusty steel in his hand?

Into the brain of this wild beast there had not penetrated, even vaguely, any idea of rights or duties. No duties, no rights or anything at all. To him, might was right; the world was a hunting wood. Only humble wretches could obey the law of labour. That's what he said: Let fools work, if they hadn't the nerve to live like men.

As the three thus conversed a man and a woman with a child in her arms passed by. They looked dejected, like famished, persecuted folk, their glance timid and awed.

"There's the workers for you," exclaimed Vidal. "That's how they are."

"The devil take them," muttered Bizco.

"Where are they bound for?" asked Manuel, eyeing them sympathetically.

"To the tile-works," answered Vidal. "To sell saffron, as we say around here."

"And why do they say that?"

"Because saffron is so dear...."

The three came to a halt and lay down upon the sod. For more than an hour they remained there, discussing women and ways and means of procuring money.

"Got any money about you?" asked Vidal of Manuel and Bizco.

"Two reales," replied the latter.

"Well, then, invite us to something," suggested Vidal. "Let's have a bottle."

Bizco assented, grumblingly, so they arose and took their way toward Madrid. A procession of whitish mules filed past them; a young, swarthy gipsy, with a long stick under his arm, mounted upon the last mule of the procession, kept shouting at every step: "Coron, coron!"

"So long, swell!" shouted Vidal to him.

"God be with all good folk," answered the gipsy in a hoarse voice. They reached a road tavern beside a ragpicker's hut, stopped, and Vidal ordered the bottle of wine.

"What's this factory?" asked Manuel, pointing to a structure at the left of the Andaluca road on the way back to Madrid.

"They make money out of blood," answered Vidal solemnly.

Manuel stared at him in fright.

"Yes. They make glue out of the blood that's left over in the slaughter-house," added his cousin, laughing.

Vidal poured the wine into the glasses and the three gulped it down.

Yonder, above the avenue of trees on the Canal, could be made out Madrid, with its long, level cluster of houses. The windows, lit up by the flush of the setting sun, glowed like live coals; in the foreground, just below San Francisco el Grande, bulked the red tanks of the gas factory with their high steel beams, amidst the obscure rubbish-heaps; from the centre of the city rose tiny towers and low chimneys which belched forth black puffs of smoke that seemed to rest motionless in the tranquil atmosphere. At one side, upon a hill, towered the Observatory, whose windows sparkled with the sun; at the other, the Guadarama range, blue with crests of white, was outlined against the clear, transparent heavens furrowed by red clouds.

"Bah," added Vidal, after a moment's silence, turning to Manuel. "You've got to come with us; we'll make a gang."

"That's the talk," stammered Bizco.

"All right. I'll see," responded Manuel unwillingly.

"What do you mean, you'll see? The gang's already formed. We'll call it the gang of The Three."

"Fine!" shouted Bizco.

"And we'll help each other?" inquired Manuel.

"Of course we will," assured his cousin. "And if any one of us should prove a traitor...."

"If any one proves a traitor," interrupted Bizco, "his guts'll be ripped out." And to lend force to his declaration he drew out his dirk and plunged it viciously into the table.

At nightfall the three returned by the road to the Toledo bridge and separated at that point, after arranging to meet on the morrow.

Manuel wondered just what he was committed to by the promise made to be a member of The Three. The life led by Bizco and Vidal frightened him. He must resolve to turn over a new leaf; but what was he to do? That was what puzzled him.

For some time Manuel did not dare to put in an appearance at the lodging-house; he would meet his mother in the street and he slept in the entry of the house where one of his sisters was employed. Later it came to pass that the landlady's niece was found in the bedroom of a neighbouring student, and this served to rehabilitate Manuel somewhat in the boarding-house.

CHAPTER II

One of the Many Disagreeable Ways of Dying in Madrid—The
Orphan—El Cojo and His Cave—Night in the Observatory.

One day Manuel was not a little surprised to learn that his mother had not been able to get up and that she was ill. For some time she had been coughing up blood, but had considered this of no importance.

Manuel presented himself humbly at the house and the landlady, instead of greeting him with recriminations, asked him in to see his mother. The only thing Petra complained of was a terrible bruised feeling all over the body and a pain in her back.

For days and days she had gone on thus, now better, now worse, until she began to run a high fever and was compelled to call in the doctor. The landlady said that they'd have to take the sick woman to the hospital; but as she was a kind-hearted soul she did not insist.

Petra had already confessed several times to the priest of the house. Manuel's sisters came from time to time, but neither brought the money necessary to the purchase of the medicines and the food that were prescribed by the doctor.

One Sunday, toward night, Petra took a turn for the worse; during the afternoon she had been conversing spiritedly with her daughters; but this animation had subsided until she was overwhelmed by a mortal collapse.

That Sunday night Doa Casiana's lodgers had an unusually succulent supper, and after the supper several ronquillas for dessert, watered by the purest concoction of the Prussian distilleries.

The spree was still in progress at ten o'clock. Petra said to Manuel:

"Call Don Jacinto and tell him that I'm worse."

Manuel went to the dining-room. He could barely make out the congested faces through the thick tobacco smoke that filled the atmosphere. As Manuel entered, one of the merrymakers said:

"A little less noise; there's somebody sick."

Manuel delivered the message to the priest.

"Your mother's scared, that's all. I'll come a little later," replied Don Jacinto.

Manuel returned to the room.

126

"Isn't he coming?" asked the sick woman.

"He'll be here right away. He says you're only scared."

"Yes. A fine scare," she murmured sadly. "Stay here."

Manuel sat down upon a trunk; he was so sleepy, he could hardly see.

He was just dozing off when his mother called to him.

"Listen," she said. "Go into the room and fetch the picture of the Virgin of Sorrows."

Manuel took down the picture,—a cheap cromograph,—and brought it to the bedroom.

"Place it at the foot of the bed so that I can see it."

The boy did as he was requested and returned to his seat. From the dining-room came a din of songs, hand-clapping and castanets.

Suddenly Manuel, who was half asleep, heard a loud, rasping sound issue from his mother's chest, and at the same time he noticed that her face had become paler than ever and was twitching strangely.

"What's the matter?"

The sufferer made no reply. Then Manuel ran to notify the priest again. Grumblingly he left the dining-room, looked at the sick woman and said to the boy:

"Your mother's dying. Stay here, and I'll be back at once with the extreme unction."

The priest ordered the merrymakers in the dining-room to cease their racket and the whole house became silent.

Nothing could be heard now save cautious footfalls, the opening and closing of doors, followed by the stertorous breathing of the dying woman and the tick-tock of the corridor clock.

The priest arrived with another who wore a stole and administered all the rites of the extreme unction. After the vicar and the sacristan had gone, Manuel looked at his mother and saw her livid features, her drooping jaw. She was dead.

The youngster was left alone in the room, which was dimly lighted by the oil lamp; there he sat on the trunk, trembling with cold and fear.

He spent the whole night thus; from time to time the landlady would enter in her underclothes and ask Manuel something or offer some bit of advice which, for the most part, he did not understand.

That night Manuel thought and suffered as perhaps he never thought and suffered at any other time; he meditated upon the usefulness of life and upon death with a perspicacity that he had never possessed. However hard he might try, he could not stem the flood of thoughts that merged one with the other.

At four in the morning the whole house was in silence, when there was heard the rattle of a latchkey in the stairway door, followed by footsteps in the corridor and then the querulous tinkling of the music-box upon the vestibule-table, playing the Mandolinata.

Manuel awoke with a start, as from a dream; he could not make out where the music was coming from; he even imagined that he had lost his head. The little organ, after several hitches and asthmatic sobs, abandoned the Mandolinata and began to roll off in double time the duet between Bettina and Pippo from *La Mascotte*:

Will you forget me, gentle swain,
Dressed in this lordly finery?

Manuel left the bedroom and asked, through the darkness:

"Who is it?"

At the same moment voices were heard from every room. The music-box cut short the duet from *La Mascotte* and launched spiritedly into the strains of Garibaldi's hymn. Suddenly the music stopped and a hoarse voice shouted:

"Paco! Paco!"

The landlady got up and asked who was making all that racket; one of the men who had just entered the house explained in a whisky-soaked voice that they were students who boarded on the third floor, and had just come from the ball in search of Paco, one of the salesmen. The landlady told them that some one had died in the house and one of the drunkards, who was a student of medicine, said he would like to view the corpse. He was persuaded to change his mind and everybody went back to his place. The next day Manuel's sisters were notified and Petra was buried....

On the day after the interment Manuel left the boarding-house and said farewell to Doa Casiana.

"What are you going to do?" she asked.

"I don't know. I'll see."

"I can't keep you here, but I don't want you to starve. Come here from time to time."

After walking about town all the morning, Manuel found himself at noon on the Ronda de Toledo, leaning against the wall of Las Americas, at a loss to know what to do with himself. To one side, likewise seated upon the turf, was a loathsome, terribly ugly, flat-nosed gamin, with a clouded eye, bare feet, and a tattered jacket through whose rents could be glimpsed his dark skin, which had been tanned by the sun and wind. Hanging from his neck was a canister into which he threw the cigarette ends that he gathered.

"Where do you live?" Manuel asked him.

"I haven't any father or mother," answered the urchin, evasively.

"What's your name?"

"The Orphan."

"And why do they call you that?"

"Why! Because I'm a foundling."

"And didn't you ever have a home?"

"No."

"And where do you sleep?"

"Well, in the summer I sleep in the caves, or in yards, and in winter, in the asphalt caldrons."

"And when they're not doing any asphalting?"

"In some shelter or other."

"All right, then. But what do you eat?"

"Whatever I'm given."

"And do you manage to do well?"

Either the foundling did not understand the question or it appeared quite silly to him, for he merely shrugged his shoulders. Manuel continued his curious interrogatory.

"Aren't your feet cold?"

"No."

"And don't you do anything?"

"Psch! ... whatever turns up. I pick up stubs, I sell sand, and when I can't earn anything I go to the Mara Cristina barracks."

"What for?"

"What for? For a meal, of course."

"And where's this barracks?"

"Near the Atocha station. Why? Would you like to go there, too?"

"Yes, I would."

"Well, let's come along then, or we'll miss mess time."

The two got up and started on their journey. The Orphan begged at the stores on the road and was given two slices of bread and a small coin.

"Will you have some, *ninchi?*" he asked, offering Manuel one of the slices.

"Hand it over."

By the Ronda de Atocha they reached the Estacin de Medioda.

"Do you know the time?" asked the Orphan.

"Yes. It's eleven."

"Well then, it's too early to go to the barracks."

Opposite the station a lady, from the seat of a coach, was making a speech proclaiming the wonders of a salve for wounds and a specific for curing the toothache.

130

The Orphan, biting away at his slice of bread, interrupted the speech of the lady in the coach, shouting ironically:

"Give me a slice to take away my toothache!"

"And another one to me!" added Manuel.

The husband of the speechmaker, an old fellow wearing a very long raglan and standing amidst the crowd of spectators listening with the greatest respect to what his better half was saying, grew indignant and speaking but half Spanish, cried:

"If I catch you your teeth'll ache for fair."

"This gentleman came from Archipipi," interrupted the Orphan.

The old codger tried to catch one of the urchins. Manuel and the Orphan ran off, dodging the man in the raglan and planting themselves opposite him.

"Impudent rascals," shouted the gentleman. "I'll give you a hiding and maybe your teeth won't really ache by the time I'm through with you."

"But they hurt already," chorused the ragamuffins.

The old fellow, exasperated beyond endurance, gave frantic chase to the urchins; a group of idlers and news-vendors jostled against him as if by accident, and the pursuer, perspiring freely and wiping his face with his handkerchief, went off in search of an officer.

"Fakir, froggie, beggar!" shouted the Orphan derisively at him.

Then, laughing at their prank, they returned to the barracks and took place at the end of a line composed of poverty-stricken folk and tramps who were waiting for a meal. An old woman who had already eaten lent them a tin in which to place their food.

They ate and then, in company of other tattered youngsters climbed the sandy slopes of San Blas hill to get a view from that spot of the soldiers on Atocha avenue.

Manuel stretched out lazily in the sun, filled with the joy of finding himself absolutely free of worriment, of gazing upon the azure sky which extended into the infinite. Such blissful comfort induced in him a deep sleep.

When he awoke it was already mid-afternoon and the wind was chasing dark clouds across the heavens. Manuel sat up; there was a knot of gamins close by, but the Orphan was nowhere to be seen.

A dense black cloud came up and blotted out the sun; shortly afterward it began to rain.

"Shall we go to Cojo's cave?" asked one of the boys.

"Come on."

The entire band of ragamuffins broke into a run in the direction of the Retiro, with Manuel hard after them. The thick raindrops fell in slanting, steel-hued lines; a stray sunbeam glittered from the sky through the dark violet clouds which were so long that they looked like huge, motionless fishes.

Ahead of the ragamuffins, at an appreciable distance, ran two women and two men.

"They're Rubia and Chata with a couple of hayseeds," said one of the gamins.

"They're running to the cave," added another.

The boys reached the top of the hill; before the entrance to the cave, which was nothing but a hole dug out of the sand, sat a one-legged man smoking a pipe.

"We're going in," announced one of the urchins to Cojo.

"You can't," he replied.

"And why not?"

"Because you can't."

"Man! Let's get in until the rain stops."

"Impossible."

"Why? Are Rubia and Chata inside?"

"What do you care if they are?"

"Shall we give those hayseeds a scare?" asked one of the ragamuffins, whose ears were covered by long black locks.

"Just try it and see," growled Cojo, seizing a rock.

"Come on to the Observatory," said another. "We won't get wet there."

132

The gang turned back, hurdled a wall that stood in their path and took refuge in the portico of the Observatory on the Atocha side. The wind was blowing from the Guadarrama range so that they were in the lee.

For the afternoon and part of the evening the rain came pouring down; they passed the time chatting about women, thefts and crimes. Two or three of these youngsters had a home to go to, but they didn't care to go. One, who was called El Marian, related a number of notable tricks and swindles; others, who displayed prodigious skill and ingenuity, roused the gathering to enthusiasm. After this theme had been exhausted, a few suggested a game of can, and the idler with the long black locks, whom they called El Canco, sang in a low feminine voice several *flamenco* songs.

At night, as it grew cold, they lay down quite close to each other upon the ground and continued their conversations. Manuel was repelled by the malevolent spirit of the gang; one of them told a story about an aged fellow of eighty, "old Rainbow," who used to sleep furtively in the Manzanares laundry in a hole formed by four mats; one night when an icy cold wind was blowing they opened two of his mats and the next day he was found frozen to death; El Marian recounted how he had been with a cousin of his, a cavalry sergeant, in a public house and how the sergeant mounted upon a naked woman's back and gashed her thighs with his spurs.

"The fact is," concluded El Marian, "there's nothing like making women suffer if you want to keep 'em satisfied."

Manuel listened in astonishment to this counsel; his mind reverted to that seamstress who came to the landlady's house, and then to Salom, and it occurred to him that he would not care to have made them love him by inflicting pain. He fell asleep with these notions whirling in his head.

When he awoke he felt the cold penetrating to his very marrow. Day was breaking and the rain had ceased; the sky, still dim, was strewn with greyish clouds. Above a hedge of shrubs shone a star in the middle of the horizon's pale band, and against this opaline glow stood out the intertwined branches of the trees, which were still without leaves.

The whistles of the locomotives could be heard from the nearby station; toward Carabanchel the lantern lights were paling in the dark fields, which could be glimpsed by the vague luminosity of nascent day.

Madrid, level, whitish, bathed in mist, rose out of the night with its many roofs, which cut the sky in a straight line; its turrets, its lofty factory chimneys; and amidst the silence of the dawn, the city and the landscape suggested the unreality and the motionlessness of a painting.

The sky became clearer, growing gradually blue. Now the new white houses stood out more sharply; the high partition-walls, pierced symmetrically by tiny windows;

the roofs, the corners, the balustrades, the red towers of recent construction, the army of chimneys, all enveloped in the cold, sad, damp, atmosphere of morning, beneath a low zinc-hued sky.

Beyond the city proper, afar, rolled the Madrilenian plain in gentle undulations, toward the mists of dawn; the Manzanares meandered along, as narrow as a band of silver; it sought the Los Angeles hill, crossing barren fields and humble districts, finally to curve and lose itself in the grey horizon. Towering above Madrid the Guadarrama loomed like a lofty blue rampart, its summits capped with snow.

In the midst of this silence a church bell began its merry pealing, but the chimes were lost in the somnolent city.

Manuel felt very cold and commenced pacing back and forth, rubbing his shoulders and his legs. Absorbed in this operation, he did not see a man in a boina, with a lantern in his hand, who approached him and asked:

"What are you doing here?"

Without replying, Manuel broke into a run down the hill; shortly afterward the rest of the gang came scurrying down, awaked by the kicks of the man in the boina.

As they reached the Velasco Museum, El Marian said:

"Let's see if we can't play a dirty trick on that damned Cojo."

"Yes. Come on."

By a side path they climbed back to the spot where they had been on the previous afternoon. From the caves of San Blas hill came a few ragamuffins crawling out on all fours; frightened by the sound of voices and thinking, doubtless, that the police had come to make a raid, they set off on a mad run, naked, with their ragged clothing under their arms.

They made their way to Cojo's cave; El Marian proposed that as a punishment for his not having let them go in the day before, they should pile a heap of grass before the entrance to the cave and set fire to the place.

"No, man, that's monstrous," objected El Canco. "The fellow hires out his cave to Rubia and Chata, who hang around here and have customers in the barracks. He has to respect his agreements with them."

"Well, we'll have to give him a lesson," retorted El Marian. "You'll see." Whereupon he crawled into the cave and reappeared soon with El Cojo's wooden leg in one hand and a stewpot in the other.

134

"Cojo! Cojo!" he shouted.

At these cries the cripple stuck his head out of the entrance to the cave, dragging himself along on his hands, bellowing blasphemies in fury.

"Cojo! Cojo!" yelled El Marian again, as if inciting a dog. "There goes your leg! And your dinner's following after!" As he spoke, he seized the wooden leg and the pot and sent them rolling down the slope.

Then they all broke into a run for the Ronda de Vallecas. Above the heights and valleys of the Pacfico district the huge red disk of the sun rose from the earth and ascended slowly and majestically behind a cluster of grimy huts.

CHAPTER III

Meeting with Roberto—Roberto Narrates the Origin of a Fantastic
  Fortune.

Manuel was compelled to return to the bakery in quest of work, and there, thanks to
Karl's intercession with the proprietor, the boy spent a while as a substitute for a
delivery-man.

Manuel understood that this was hardly a suitable thing for him as a regular position,
and that it would get him nowhere; but he was at a loss what to do, what road to take.

When he was left without a job, he managed to exist as long as he had enough to pay
for a chop-house meal. There came a day when he was stranded without a cntimo
and he resorted to the Mara Cristina barracks.

For two or three days he had been taking up his position among the beggars of the
breadline, when once he caught sight of Roberto entering the barracks. He did not
go over to him, as he feared to lose his place, but after eating he waited until Roberto
came out.

"Don Roberto!" hailed Manuel.

The student turned deathly pale; at sight of Manuel he regained his composure.

"What are you doing here?" he asked.

"You can see for yourself. I come here to eat. I can't find work."

"Ah! You come here to eat?"

"Yes, sir."

"Well, I come for the same reason," murmured Roberto, laughing.

"You?"

"Yes. I have been cheated out of my rightful fortune."

"And what are you doing now?"

"I'm working on a newspaper, waiting until there's a vacancy. At the barracks I
made friends with a sculptor who comes here for his meals, too, and we both live in a

garret. I laugh at such things, for I am convinced that some day I'm going to be wealthy, and when I am, I'll recall these hard times with pleasure."

"He's beginning to rave already," thought Manuel.

"Then you don't believe that I'm going to be a rich man some day?"

"Certainly. Of course I do!"

"Where are you going?" asked Roberto.

"Nowhere in particular."

"Let's take a stroll."

"Come on."

They walked down to Alfonso XII Street and went into the Retiro; when they had gone as far as the end of the carriage drive they sat down on a bench.

"We'll drive along here in a carriage when I become a millionaire," said Roberto.

"You mean you.... As for me...." replied Manuel.

"You, too. Do you imagine that I'm going to let you stand in the barrack's bread line when I have my millions?"

"He's truly a bit off his base," thought Manuel, "but he has a kind heart." Then he added. "Have your affairs been making much progress?"

"No, not much. The question is still pretty well tangled. But it will be straightened out, mark my word."

"Do you know that that circus chap with the phonograph showed up one day with a woman named Rosa?" said Manuel. "I went hunting for you to see whether she was the one you were talking about."

"No. The one I was looking for is dead."

"Then your case is all cleared up?"

"Yes. But I need money. Don Telmo was ready to lend me ten thousand duros on condition that I'd give him half of the fortune as soon as I entered into possession of it, if I won. But I refused."

137

"How foolish."

"What's more, he wants me to marry his niece."

"And you didn't want to?"

"No."

"But she's pretty."

"Yes. But she's not to my taste."

"What? Are you still thinking of the Baroness's daughter?"

"How could I forget her! I've seen her. She is exquisite."

"Yes. She's certainly good-looking."

"Only good-looking! Don't blaspheme. The moment I saw her, my mind was made up. It's sink or swim for me."

"You run the risk of being left with nothing."

"I know that. I don't care. All or nothing. The Hastings have always been men of will and resolution. And I'm inspired by the example of one of my relatives. It's an invigorating case of pertinacity. You'll see."

"My uncle, the brother of my grandfather, was employed in a London business house and learned, through a sailor, that a chest filled with silver had been dug up on one of the islands in the Pacific; it was supposed that it came from a vessel that had left Peru for the Philippines. My uncle succeeded in finding out the exact spot where the ship had been wrecked, and at once he gave up his position and went off to the Philippines. He chartered a brig, reached the spot indicated,—a reef of the Magellan archipelago,—they sounded at several points and after hard work dredged up only a few shattered chests that contained not a trace of anything. When their food supply gave out they were forced to return, and my uncle reached Manila without a farthing. He got a position in a business house. After a year of this a fellow from the United States proposed that they should go out together in quest of the treasure, and my uncle accepted, on the condition that they'd share the profits equally. On this second voyage they brought up two huge, very heavy chests, one filled with silver ingots, the other with Mexican gold pieces. The Yankee and my uncle divided the money and each one's share amounted to more than one hundred thousand duros. But my uncle, who was an obstinate fellow, returned to the site of the shipwreck and this time he must have located the treasure, for he came back to England with a colossal fortune. Today the Hastings, who still live in England, are millionaires. Do you remember that Fanny who came to the tavern in Las Injurias with us?"

"Yes."

"Well, she's one of the wealthy Hastings of England."

"Then why didn't you ask them for some money?" queried Manuel.

"No, never. Not even if I were dying of hunger, and this despite the fact that they've often offered to help me. Before coming to Madrid I sailed almost around the world in a yacht belonging to Fanny's brother."

"And this fortune that you expect to own, is it also on some island?" asked Manuel.

"It seems to me that you're of the kind that have no faith," answered Roberto. "Before the crowing of the cock you would deny me three times."

"No. I know nothing of your affairs; but if you should ever need me, I'll be ready to serve you, and gladly."

"But you doubt my destiny, and are wrong to do so. You imagine that I'm a bit daft."

"No, no, sir."

"Bah! You think that this fortune that I'm to inherit is all a hoax."

"I don't know."

"Well, it isn't. The fortune exists. Do you remember I was once talking with Don Telmo, in your presence, about a conversation I had with a certain book-binder in his house?"

"Yes, sir. I remember."

"Well, that conversation furnished me with the clew to all the investigations I afterward conducted; I won't tell you how I went about collecting data and more data, little by little, for that would bore you. I'll put the thing for you in a nutshell."

As he finished his sentence Roberto arose from the bench upon which they were seated and said to Manuel:

"Let's be going; that fellow yonder is hanging around trying to hear what we're talking about."

Manuel got up, surer than ever that Roberto was crazy on that point; they walked by El Angel Cado, reached the Meteorological Observatory and from there left for the hills that lie opposite the Pacfico and the Doa Carlota districts.

"We can talk here," murmured Roberto. "If any one comes along, let me know."

"Don't worry on that score," assured Manuel.

"Well, as I was telling you, that conversation provided the foundation of a fortune that will soon be mine; but see how clumsy a fellow can be and how ill things look when they're too near. Until a full year after I had had that conversation I made no attempt to start my case. The first efforts I made about two years ago. The idea came to me on one Carnival day. I was giving lessons in English and studying at the University; of the little money I earned I had to send some to my mother and the rest went toward my upkeep and my tuition fees. This Carnival day,—a Tuesday, I remember,—I had no more than three pesetas to my name; I had been working so hard and so steadily, without a moment's let-up, that I said to myself: 'Yes, sir. Today I'm going to do something foolish. I'm going to disguise myself. And surely enough, on San Marcos Street I hired a domino and a mask for three pesetas, and I went out on to the street with not a cntimo in my pocket. I began to walk down toward La Castellana and as I reached the Cibeles fountain I stopped and asked myself in astonishment: 'Why did I have to spend the little money I had on me for a disguise, when I know nobody anyway?'

"I was about to return and get rid of my disguise, but there were so many people in the crowd that I had to float with the tide. I don't know whether you've ever noticed how lonesome one feels on these Carnival days amidst the throngs of people. This solitude in the crowd is far more intense than solitude in a forest. It brought to my mind the thousand absurdities one commits; the sterility of my own life. 'I'm going to waste my life in some grubbing profession,' I said to myself. 'I'll wind up by becoming a teacher, a sort of English instructress. No; never that. I must seek an opportunity and the means to emancipate myself from this petty existence, or else plunge into tragic life.' It also occurred to me that it was very possible that the opportunity had come to me without my knowing how to take advantage of it, and at once I recalled my conversation with that book-binder. I decided to go into the matter until I saw it more clearly. Without any hope, you'll understand, but simply as an exercise of the will. 'I need more will-power,' I said to myself, 'with which to conquer the details that come up every moment rather than to perform some great sacrifice or be capable of an instant of abnegation. Sublime moments, heroic acts, are rather the deeds of an exalted intelligence than of the will; I have always felt it in me to perform some great deed such as taking a trench or defending a barricade or going to the North Pole; but, would I be capable of finishing a daily stint, composed of petty provocations and dull routine? Yes,' said I to myself, and with this resolution I mingled with the masked merrymakers and returned to Madrid while the rest were at the height of their fun."

"And have you been working ever since?"

140

"Ever since, and with rapid persistency. The book-binder didn't care to give me any details, so I installed myself in the Casa de Cannigos, asked for the Libro de Turnos and there from day to day I'd look over list after list until I found the date of the lawsuit; from there I went to Las Salesas, located the archive and I spent an entire month in a garret opening dockets until I found the documents. Then I had to get baptismal certificates, seek recommendations from a bishop, run hither and thither, intrigue, scurry to this place and that, until the question began to clear up, and with all my documents properly arranged I presented my claim at London. During these two years I laid the foundations for the tower to the top of which I'll climb yet."

"And are you sure that the foundations are solid?"

"Certainly. They're all facts. Here they are," and Roberto drew from his pocket a folded paper. "This is the genealogical tree of my family. This red circle is Don Fermn Nez de Latona, priest of Labraz, who goes to Venezuela at the end of the seventeenth century, and returns to Spain during the Trafalgar epoch. On his journey home an English vessel captures the Spanish ship on which the priest is sailing and takes him and the other passengers prisoner, transporting them to England. Don Fermn reclaims his fortune of the English government, it is returned to him and he deposits it in the Bank of England, and sails back to Spain during the War of Independence. As money was none too safe in Spain at that time, Don Fermn leaves his fortune in the Bank of England, and on one occasion, desiring to withdraw a large sum for the purchase of certain estates, he goes to England with a cousin's niece;— the cousin was his only relation and was named Juan Antonio. This niece—" and Roberto pointed to a circle upon the sheet, "marries an Irish gentleman, Bandon, and dies after three years. The priest Don Fermn decides to return to Spain and orders his fortune to be remitted to the San Fernando Bank, but before the money is transferred Don Fermn dies. Bandon, the Irishman, presents a will in which the priest names his niece as sole heir, and proves, moreover, that he had a son by his wife, who died directly after baptism. Don Fermn's cousin, Juan Antonio, of Labraz, brings suit against Bandon, and the suit lasts for nearly twenty years. Juan Antonio dies and the Irishman is thus enabled to collect part of the inheritance.

"Juan Antonio's other daughter marries a cousin of hers, a merchant of Haro, and has three children, two boys and a girl. The girl enters a nunnery, one of the boys dies in the Carlist war and the other goes into business and leaves for America.

"This fellow, Juan Manuel Nnez makes a regular fortune and marries a native and has two daughters: Augusta and Margarita. Augusta, the younger, marries my father, Ricardo Hasting, who was a madcap and ran away from his home; Margarita weds a soldier, colonel Buenavida. They all come to Spain with plenty of money; my father plunges into disastrous business schemes, and after he has been utterly ruined he learns, I don't know how, that the fortune of the priest Nez de Latona is at the disposition of the heirs. He goes to England, enters his claim; they demand his documents, he brings forth the baptismal records of his wife's ancestors and it is found that the priest Don Fermin's birth registration is missing. Soon my father gives up writing and years and years go by; at the end of more than ten we receive a letter telling us that he has died in Australia.

"Margarita, my mother's sister, is left a widow with a daughter, marries a second time, and her husband turns out a rascal of the worst brand who leaves her without a cntimo. Rosa, the daughter of the first marriage, unable to put up with her step-father, elopes with an actor and nothing more is heard of her.

"If," added Roberto, "you have followed my explanations, you will have seen that the only remaining relatives of Don Fermn Nez de Latona are my sisters and I, because Margarita's daughter Rosa Nez has died.

"Now, the point is to prove this relationship, and this relationship is proved, for I have the baptismal documents that show our descent in a direct line from Juan Antonio, Fermn's brother. But why doesn't Fermn Ncz de Latona's name appear in the parish register of Labraz? That's what's been bothering me, and I've settled it. That Irishman Bandon, when his rival Juan Antonio died, sent to Spain an agent named Shaphter, who caused the disappearance of Don Fermn's baptismal certificate. How? I don't know as yet. In the meantime, I'm continuing the claim in London, just to keep the case in the courts, and the Hastings are the ones who are pushing the suit."

"And how much does this fortune amount to?" asked Manuel.

"Reckoning principal and interest, to a million pounds sterling."

"And is that much?"

"Without allowing for exchange, about one hundred million reales; allowing for exchange, a hundred and thirty."

Manuel burst out laughing.

"And all for you alone?"

"For me and my sisters. You can just imagine, when I collect that sum, what these cheap carriages and such things will mean to me. Nothing at all."

"And now, in the meantime, you haven't a peseta."

"Such is life. You've got to wait. It can't be helped. Now, when nobody believes me, I enjoy the recognition of my own strength more than I'll enjoy my subsequent triumph. I have reared a whole mountain; a dense mist prevents people from seeing it; tomorrow the clouds will scatter and the mountain will stand forth with snow-crowned crests."

142

Manuel thought it silly to be talking of all this opulence when neither of them had enough to buy a meal. Pretending important matters, he took leave of Roberto.

CHAPTER IV,

Dolores the Scandalous—Pastiri's Tricks—Tender Savagery—A
Modest Out-of-the-way Robbery.

After a week spent in sleeping in the open Manuel decided one day to rejoin Vidal
and Bizco and to take up their evil ways.

He inquired after his friends in the taverns on the Andaluca cart-road, at La Llorosa,
Las Injurias, and a chum of El Bizco, who was named El Chingui, told him that El
Bizco was staying at Las Cambroneras, at the home of a well-known thieving
strumpet called Dolores the Scandalous.

Manuel went off to Las Cambroneras, asked for Dolores and was shown a door in a
patio inhabited by gipsies.

Manuel knocked, but Dolores refused to open the door; finally, after hearing the
boy's explanations, she allowed him to come in.

Dolores' home consisted of a room about three metres square; in the rear could be
made out a bed where El Bizco was sleeping in his clothes, beside a sort of vaulted
niche with a chimney and a tiny fireplace. The furnishings of the room consisted of
a table, a trunk, a white shelf containing plates and earthenware pots, and a pine
wall-bracket that supported an oil-lamp.

Dolores was a woman of about fifty; she wore black clothes, a red kerchief knotted
around her forehead like a bandage and another of some indistinct colour over her
head.

Manuel called to El Bizco and, when the cross-eyed fellow awoke, asked after Vidal.

"He'll be here right away," said El Bizco, and then, turning upon the old lady, he
growled: "Hey, you, fetch my boots."

Dolores was slow in executing his orders, whereupon El Bizco, wishing to show off
his domination over the woman, struck her.

The woman did not even mumble; Manuel looked coldly at El Bizco, in disgust; the
other averted his gaze.

"Want a bite?" asked El Bizco of Manuel when he had got out of bed.

"If you have anything good...."

Dolores drew from the fire a pan filled with meat and potatoes.

144

"You take good care of yourselves," murmured Manuel, whom hunger had made profoundly cynical.

"They trust us at the butcher's," said Dolores, to explain the abundance of meat.

"If you and I didn't work hard hereabouts," interjected El Bizco, "much we'd be eating."

The woman smiled modestly. They finished their lunch and Dolores produced a bottle of wine.

"This woman," declared El Bizco, "just as you behold her there, beats them all. Show him what we have in the corner."

"Not now, man."

"And why not?"

"Suppose some one should come?"

"I'll bolt the door."

"All right."

El Bizco bolted the door. Dolores pushed the table to the middle of the room, went over to the wall, pulled away a scrap of kalsomined canvas about a yard square, and revealed a gap crammed with ribbons, cords, lace edging and other objects of passementerie.

"How's that?" said El Bizco. "And it's all of her own collecting."

"You must have quite a bit of money there."

"Yes. It's worth quite a bit," agreed Dolores. Then she let the strip of canvas fall into place against the excavation in the wall, fastened it and drew up the bed before it. El Bizco unbolted the door. In a few moments there was a knock.

"That must be Vidal," said El Bizco, adding in a low voice, as he turned to Manuel, "See here, not a word to him."

Vidal strutted in with his carefree air, expressed his pleasure at Manuel's coming, and the three left for the street.

"Are you going to be around here?" asked the old woman.

"Yes."

"Don't come late, then, eh?" added Dolores, addressing Bizco.

The cross-eyed bully did not deign to make any reply.

The three chums went to the square that faces Toledo bridge; near by, at a stand owned by Garatusa, a penitentiary graduate who ran a "fence" for thieves and didn't lose any money at it, they had a drink and then, walking along Ocho Hilos Avenue they came to the Ronda de Toledo.

The vicinity of El Rastro was thronged with Sunday crowds.

Along the wall of Las Grandiosas Amricas, in the space between the Slaughter-house and the Veterinary School, a long row of itinerant hawkers had set up their stands.

Some, garbed like beggars, stood dozing motionless against the wall, indifferently contemplating their wares: old pictures, new chromographs, books; useless, damaged, filthy articles which they felt sure none of the public would purchase. Others were gesticulating and arguing with their customers; several repulsive, grimy old women with huge straw hats on their heads, dirty hands, arms akimbo and indecencies quivering upon their lips, were chattering away like magpies.

The gipsy women in their motley garments were combing their little brunettes and their black-skinned, large-eyed *churumbeles* in the sun; a knot of vagrants was carrying on a serious discussion; mendicants wrapped in rags, maimed, crippled, were shouting, singing, wailing, and the Sunday throng, in search of bargains, scurried back and forth, stopping now and then to question, to pry, while folks passed by with faces congested by the heat of the sun,—a spring sun that blinded one with the chalky reflection of the dusty soil, glittering and sparkling with a thousand glints in the broken mirrors and the metal utensils displayed in heaps upon the ground. To add to this deafening roar of cries and shouts, two organs pierced the air with the merry wheeze of their blending, interweaving tones.

Manuel, El Bizco and Vidal strolled to the head of El Rastro and turned down again. At the door of Las Amricas they met Pastiri sniffing around the place.

Catching sight of Manuel and the other two, the fellow of the three cards approached and said:

"Shall we have some wine?"

"Sure."

They entered one of the taverns of the Ronda. Pastiri was alone that day, as his companion had gone off to the Escorial; since he had no one to act as his confederate in the game he hadn't made a cntimo. Now, if they would consent to act as bait to induce the inquisitive onlookers to play, he'd give them a share of the profits.

"Ask him how much?" said El Bizco to Vidal.

"Don't be an idiot."

Pastiri explained the matter for El Bizco's benefit; the confederates were to place bets and then proclaim in a loud voice that they had won. Then he'd see to making the spectators eager to play.

"All right. We know what to do," said Vidal.

"You agree to the scheme?"

"Yes, man."

Pastiri gave them three pesetas apiece and the four left the tavern, crossed the Ronda and made their way in the crowds of El Rastro.

Every once in a while Pastiri would stop, thinking he had caught sight of a prospective dupe; El Bizco or Manuel would place a bet; but the fellow who looked like an easy victim would smile as he saw them lay the snare or else pass on indifferently, quite accustomed to this type of trickery.

Soon Pastiri noticed a group of rustics with their broad hats and short trousers.

"*Aluspiar*, here come a few birds and we may work them for something," he said, and he planted himself and his card table directly in the path of the country-folk and began his game.

El Bizco bet two pesetas and won; Manuel followed suit with the same results.

"This fellow is a cinch," said Vidal in a loud voice, turning to the group of hayseeds. "Have you seen all the money he's losing? That soldier there just won six duros."

Hearing this, one of the rustics drew near, and seeing that Manuel and El Bizco were winning, he wagered a peseta and won. The fellow's companions advised him to retire with his winnings; but his greed got the best of him and he returned to bet two pesetas, losing them.

Then Vidal bet a duro.

"Here's a five-peseta piece," he declared, ringing the coin upon the ground, He picked out the right card and won.

Pastiri made a gesture of anoyance.

The rustic wagered another duro and lost; he glanced anxiously at his fellow countrymen, extracted another duro and lost that, too.

At this moment a guard happened along and the group broke up; noting Pastiri's movement of flight, the hayseed tried to seize him, grabbing at his coat, but the trickster gave a rude tug and escaped in the crowd.

Manuel, Vidal and El Bizco made their way across the Plaza del Rastro to Embajadores Street.

El Bizco had four pesetas, Manuel six and Vidal fourteen.

"And what are we going to return to that guy?" asked El Bizco.

"Return? Nothing," answered Vidal.

"Why, that would be robbing him of his whole year's profits," objected Manuel.

"What of it? Deuce take him," retorted Vidal. "We came darn near getting caught ourselves, with nothing for our trouble."

It was lunch hour and they wondered where to go; Vidal settled it, saying that as long as they were on Embajadores Street, the Society of the Three, in plenary session, might as well continue on the way down till they got to La Manigua restaurant.

The suggestion was accepted and the associates spent that Sunday afternoon in royal fashion; Vidal was splendid, spending Pastiri's money right and left, inviting several girls to their table and dancing all the *chulo* steps.

To Manuel this beginning of his free life seemed not at all bad. At night the three comrades, somewhat the worse for wine, ambled up Embajadores Street, turning into the surrounding road.

"Where am I going to sleep?" asked Manuel.

"Come over to my house," answered Vidal.

When they came in sight of Casa Blanca, El Bizco left them.

"Thank the Lord that tramp has gone," muttered Vidal.

148

"Have you had a scrap with him?"

"He's a beastly fellow. He lives with La Escandalosa, who's an old fox in truth, sixty years at the very least, and spends everything she robs with her lovers. But she feeds him and he ought to have some consideration for her. Nothing doing, though; he's always kicking her and punching her and pricking her with his dirk, and one time he even heated an iron and wanted to burn her. If he takes her money, well and good; but what's the sense of his burning her?"

They reached Casa Blanca, a squalid section consisting of a single street; Vidal opened a door with his key; he lighted a match and the pair climbed up to a tiny room with a mattress placed on the bricks.

"You'll have to sleep on the floor," said Vidal. "This bed belongs to my girl."

"All right."

"Take this for your head," and he threw him a woman's rolled-up skirt.

Manuel pillowed his head against the skirt and fell asleep. He awoke at dawn. He opened his eyes and sat down upon the floor without a thought as to where he might be. Through a tiny window came a pale glow. Vidal, stretched out on the mattress, was snoring; beside him slept a girl, breathing with her mouth wide open; long streaks of rouge stained her cheeks.

Manuel felt nauseated by the excess of the previous day's drink; he was deeply dejected. He gave serious thought to his life-problems.

"I'm not made for this," he told himself. "I'm neither a savage like Bizco nor a brazen, carefree lout like Vidal. What am I going to do, then?"

A thousand things occurred to him, for the most part impossible of attainment; he imagined all manner of involved projects. Within him, vaguely, his maternal inheritance, with its respect for all established custom, struggled against his anti-social, vagrant instincts that were fed by his mode of living.

"Vidal and Bizco," he said to himself, "are luckier chaps than myself. They don't hesitate; they have no scruples. They've got a start on their careers...."

In the end, he considered, they would come to the gallows or to the penitentiary; but in the meantime the one experienced no suffering because he was too beastly to know what it meant, and the other because he was too lazy, and both of them let themselves float tranquilly with the stream.

Despite his scruples and his remorse, Manuel spent the summer under the protection of El Bizco and Vidal, living in Casa Blanca with his cousin and his cousin's mistress, a girl who sold newspapers and practised thievery at the same time.

The Society of the Three carried on its operations in the suburbs and Las Ventas, La Prosperidad and the Doa Carlota section, the Vallecas bridge and the Four Roads; and if the existence of this society never came to be suspected and never figured in the annals of crime, it is because its misdemeanours were limited to modest burglaries of the sort facilitated by the carelessness of property owners.

The three associates were not content to operate in the suburbs of Madrid; they extended the radius of their activities to the nearby towns and to all places in general where crowds came together.

The market and the small squares were test localities, for the booty might be of a larger quantity but on the other hand the police were especially vigilant.

In general, they exploited the laundries more than any other place.

Vidal, like the clever fellow he was, managed to Convince El Bizco that he was the most gifted of the three for the work. The cross-eyed thug, out of sheer vanity, always undertook the most difficult part of the task, seizing the booty, while Vidal and Manuel kept a sharp lookout.

Vidal would say to Manuel, at the very moment of the robbery, when El Bizco already had the stolen sheet or chemise under his coat:

"If anyone happens along, don't say a word; nothing. Let them arrest him; we'll shut up tight as clams, absolutely motionless; if they ask anything, we know nothing. Right-o?"

"Agreed."

Sheets, chemises, cloaks and all the other articles they robbed they would sell at the second-hand shop on La Ribera de Curtidores, which Don Telmo used to visit. The owner, employ or whatever he was of the shop, would purchase everything the thieves brought, at a very low price.

This "fence," which profited by the oversight of some base officer (for the police lists did not bother with these things), was presided over by a fellow called Uncle Prquique. He spent his whole life passing to and fro in front of his establishment. To deceive the municipal guard he sold shoe-laces and bargains that came from the old-clothes shop he conducted.

In the spring this fellow would don a cook's white cap and cry out his tarts with a word that he scarcely pronounced and which he liked to alter constantly. Sometimes the word seemed to be Prquique! Prquique! but at once it would change sound and be transformed into Prqueque or Prquique, and these phonetic modifications were extended to infinity.

The origin of this word Prquique, which cannot be found in the dictionary, was as follows: The cream tarts sold by the man in the white cap brought five cntimos apiece and he would cry "*A perra chica! A perra Chica!* Only five pesetas apiece! A five-peseta piece!" As a result of his lazy enunciation he suppressed the first A and converted the other two into E, thus transforming his cry into "*Perre chique! Perre chique!*" Later, *Perre chique* turned into *Prquique*.

The "fence" guard, a jolly soul, was a specialist in crying wares; he shaded his cries most artistically; he would go from the highest notes to the lowest or vice versa. He would begin, for example, on a very high note, shouting:

"Look here! A real! Only one real! Ladies' and gents' hosiery at a real a pair! Look-a-here now! A real a pair!" Then, lowering his register, he would continue, gravely: "A nice Bayonne waistcoat. A splendid bargain!" And as a finale, he would add in a basso profundo: "Only twenty pesetas!"

Uncle Prquique knew the Society of the Three, and he would favour El Bizco and Vidal with his advice.

Safer and more profitable than dealing with the stolen-goods purchasers of the second-hand shop was the plan followed by Dolores la Escandalosa, who sold the ribbons and the lace that she pilfered to itinerant hawkers who paid very well. But the members of the Society of the Three were eager to get their dividends quickly.

The sale completed, the three would repair to a tavern at the end of Embajadores avenue, corner of Las Delicias, which they called the Handkerchief Corner.

The associates were especially careful not to rob twice in the same place and never to appear together in those vicinities where unfavourable surveillance was suspected.

Some days, which did not come often, when theft brought no plunder, the three companions were compelled to work in the Campillo del Mundo Nuevo, scattering heaps of wood and gathering it together with rakes after it had been properly aired and dried.

Another of the Society's means of subsistence was cat-hunting. El Bizco, who was endowed with no talent (his head, as Vidal said, was a salted melon) had a really great gift for catching cats. All he needed was a sack and a stick and he did famously. Every living cat in sight was soon in his game-bag.

The members made no distinction between slender or consumptive cats, or pregnant tabbies. Every puss that came along was devoured with the same ravenous appetite.

They would sell the skins in El Rastro; when there were no ready funds, the innkeeper of the Handkerchief Corner would let them have wine and bread on tick, and the Society would indulge in a Sardanapalesque banquet....

One afternoon in August Vidal, who had dined in Las Ventas the previous day with his girl, proposed to his comrades a scheme to rob an abandoned house on the East Road.

The project was discussed in all seriousness, and on the afternoon of the following day the three went out to look the territory over.

It was Sunday, there was a bull-fight; omnibuses and street cars, packed with people, rolled along Alcal Street beside open hacks occupied by harlots in Manila mantles and men of knavish mien.

Outside the bull-ring the throng was denser than ever; from the street cars came pouring streams of people who ran for the entrance; the ticket-speculators rushed upon them with a shout; amidst the black multitude shone the white helmets of the mounted guards. From the inside of the ring came a muffled roar like the tide.

Vidal, El Bizco and Manuel, chagrined that they could not go in, continued on their way, passed Las Ventas and took the road to Viclvaro. The south wind, warm and sultry, laid a white sheet of dust over the fields; along the road from different directions drove black and white hearses, for adults and children respectively, followed by gigs containing mourners.

Vidal indicated the house: it stood back from the road and seemed abandoned. It was fronted by a garden with its gate; behind extended an orchard planted with leafless saplings, with a water-mill. The orchard-wall was low and could be scaled with relative facility; no danger threatened; there were neither prying neighbours nor dogs; the nearest house, a marbler's workshop, was more than three hundred metres distant.

From the neighbourhood of the house could be made out the East cemetery, girded by arid yellow fields and barren hillocks; in the opposite direction rose the Bull Ring with its bright banner and the outlying houses of Madrid. The dusty road to the burial-ground ran between ravines and green slopes, among abandoned tile-kilns and excavations that showed the reddish ochre bowels of the earth.

After a minute examination of the house and its surroundings, the three returned to Las Ventas. At night they felt like going back to Madrid, but Vidal suggested that they had better remain where they were, so that they could commit the robbery at dawn of the next day. This was decided upon and they lay down in a tile-kiln, in the passageway formed by two walls of heaped-up bricks.

A cold wind blew violently throughout the night. Manuel was the first to awake and he roused the other two. They left the passageway formed by the walls of bricks. It was still night; from time to time a segment of the moon peered through the dark clouds; now it hid, now it seemed to rest upon the bosom of one of those dense clouds which it silvered so delicately.

In the distance, above Madrid a bright glow began to appear, irradiated by the lights of the city; a few tombstones in the cemetery cast a pallid shimmer.

Dawn was already tinting the heavens with its melancholy flush when the three robbers approached the house.

Manuel's heart was pounding with agitation.

"Ah, by the way," said Vidal. "If by any accident we should be surprised, we mustn't run; we've got to stick right in the house."

El Bizco burst into laughter; Manuel, who knew that his cousin wasn't talking just for the sake of hearing his voice, asked:

"Why?"

"Because if they catch us in the house it's only a balked attempt at robbery, and the punishment isn't severe; on the other hand, if they catch us in flight, that would be a successful robbery and the penalty would be great. So I was told yesterday."

"Well, I'll escape if I can."

"Do as you please."

They scaled the wall; Vidal remained astride of it, leaning forward and watching for signs of any one. Manuel and El Bizco, making their way astraddle along the wall, approached the house and, entrusting their feet to the roof of a shed, jumped down to a terrace with a bower slightly higher than the orchard.

The rear door and the balconies of the ground floor led to this gallery; but both the door and the balconies were so well fastened that it was impossible to open them.

"Can't you make it?" whispered Vidal from his perch.

"No."

"Here, take my knife." And Vidal threw it dawn to the gallery.

Manuel tried to pry the balconies open with the knife but met with no success; El Bizco attempted to force the door with his shoulder and it yielded enough to leave a chink, whereupon Manuel introduced the blade of the knife and worked the catch of the lock back until he could open the door. El Bizco and Manuel then went in.

The lower floor of the house consisted of a vestibule, which formed the bottom of a staircase leading to a corridor, and two rooms whose balconies overlooked the orchard.

The first thing that came to Manuel's head was to open the lock of the door that led to the road.

"Now," said El Bizco to him, after admiring this prudent precaution, "let's see what there is in the place."

They set about calmly and deliberately to take an inventory of the house; there wasn't three ochavos' worth of material in the entire establishment. They were forcing the dining-room closet when of a sudden they heard the bark of a dog close by and they ran in fright to the gallery.

"What's the matter?" they asked Vidal.

"A damned dog's begun to bark and he'll certainly attract somebody's attention."

"Throw a stone at him."

"Where'll I get it?"

"Scare him."

"He'll bark all the more."

"Jump down here, or they'll surely see you."

Vidal jumped down into the orchard. The dog, who must have been a moral animal and a defender of private property, continued his loud barking.

"But the deuce!" growled Vidal at his friends. "Haven't you finished yet?"

"There's nothing!"

The three returned to the rooms trembling; they seized a napkin and stuffed into it whatever they laid hands upon: a copper clock, a white metal candlestick, a broken electric bell, a mercury barometer, a magnet and a toy cannon.

154

Vidal climbed up the wall with the bundle.

"Here he is," he whispered in fright.

"Who?"

"The dog."

"I'll go down first," mumbled Manuel, and placing the knife between his teeth he let himself drop. The dog, instead of setting upon him, withdrew a short distance, but he continued his barking.

Vidal did not dare to jump down with the bundle in his hands; so he threw it carefully upon some bushes; as it fell, only the barometer broke; the rest was already broken. El Bizco and Vidal then jumped down and the three associates set out on a cross-country run, pursued by the canine defender of private property, who barked at their heels.

"What damned fools we are!" exclaimed Vidal, stopping. "If a guard should see us running like this he'd certainly arrest us."

"And if we pass the city gate they'll recognize what we're carrying in this bundle and we'll be stopped," added Manuel.

The Society halted to deliberate and choose a course of action. The booty was left at the foot of a wall. They lay down on the ground.

"A great many rag-dealers and dustmen pass this way," said Vidal, "on the road to La Elipa. Let's offer this to the first one that comes along."

"For three duros," corrected El Bizco.

"Why, of course."

They waited a while and soon a ragpicker hove into view, bearing an empty sack and headed for Madrid. Vidal called him over and offered to sell their bundle.

"What'll you give us for these things?"

The ragdealer looked over the contents of the bundle, made a second inventory, and then in a jesting tone, with a rough voice, asked:

"Where did you steal this?"

The three associates chorused their protestation, but the ragpicker paid no heed.

"I can't give you more than three pesetas for the whole business."

"No," answered Vidal. "Rather than accept that we'll take the bundle with us."

"All right. The first guard I meet I'll inform against you and tell him that you're carrying stolen goods on your person."

"Come across with the three pesetas," said Vidal. "Take the bundle."

Vidal took the money and the ragdealer, laughing, took the package.

"The first guard we see we'll tell that you've got stolen goods in your sack," shouted Vidal to the ragdealer. The man with the sack got angry and gave chase to the trio.

"Hey there! Come back! Come back!" he bellowed.

"What do you want?"

"Give me my three pesetas and take your bundle."

"Nix. Give us a duro and we won't say a word."

"Like hell."

"Give us only two pesetas more."

"Here's one, you rascal."

Vidal seized the coin that the ragdealer threw at him, and, as none was sure of himself, they made off hurriedly. When they reached Dolores' house in Las Cambroneras, they were bathed in perspiration, exhausted.

They ordered a flask of wine from the tavern, "A rotten bungle we made of it, hang it all," grumbled Vidal.

After the wine was paid for there remained ten reales; this they divided among the three, receiving eighty cntimos apiece. Vidal summed up the day's work with the remark that this committing robberies in out-of-the-way spots was all disadvantages and no advantages, for besides exposing oneself to the danger of being sent to the penitentiary almost for life and getting a beating and being chewed up by a moral dog, a fellow ran the risk of being wretchedly fooled.

CHAPTER V

Gutter Vestals—The Troglodytes.

"No use. We've got to get rid of that beastly Bizco. Every time I see him hate him more and he disgusts me more."

"Why?"

"Because he's a brute. Let him go off to his old fox, Dolores. You and I can go to the theatre every night."

"How?"

"With the claque. We don't have to pay. All we have to do is applaud when we get the signal."

This condition seemed to Manuel so easy to fulfil that he asked his cousin:

"But listen. How is it, then, that everybody doesn't go to the theatre like that?"

"Because they don't all know the head of the claque as I do."

And as a matter of fact they went to the Apollo. For the first few days all Manuel could do was think of the plays and the actresses. Vidal, with his superior manner in all things, learned the songs right away; Manuel secretly envied him.

Between the acts the members of the claque would adjourn to a tavern on Barquillo Street, varying this occasionally with a visit to another place on the Plaza, del Rey. This latter resort was the rendezvous of the claquers that worked in Price's Circus.

Almost all the legion of applauders were youngsters; a few of them worked in shops here and there; for the most part they were loafers and organgrinders who wound up by becoming supernumeraries, chorus men or ticket-speculators.

There were among them effeminate, clean-shaven types with a woman's face and a shrill voice.

At the entrance to the theatre Vidal and Manuel made the acquaintance of a group of girls, from thirteen to eighteen years of age, who wandered about Alcal Street approaching well-to-do pillars of the middle class; they pretended to be news-vendors and always had a copy of the *Heraldo* with them.

Vidal cultivated the intimacy of the girls; they were almost all homely, but this did not interfere with his plans, which consisted of extending the radius of his activities and his knowledge.

"We must leave the suburbs and work our way toward the centre," said Vidal.

Vidal wished Manuel to help him, but Manuel had no gift for it. Vidal came to be the cadet for four girls who lived together in Cuatro Caminos and were named, respectively, La Mella, La Goya, La Rabanitos and Engracia; they had come to form, together with Vidal, El Bizco and Manuel another Society, though this one was anonymous.

The poor girls needed protection; they were pursued more than the other loose women by the police because they paid no graft to the inspectors. They would be forever fleeing from the guards and agents, who, whenever there was a round-up, would take them to the station and thence to the Convento de las Trinitarias.

The thought of being immured in the convent struck genuine terror into their hearts.

"To think of never seeing the street," they moaned, as if this were a most horrible punishment.

And the abandonment at night in the unprotected thoroughfares, which inspired horror in others; the cold, the rain, the snow,—were to them liberty and life.

They all spoke in a rough manner; their grammar and word-forms were incorrect; language in them leaped backwards into a curious atavic regression.

They spiced their talk with a long string of theatrical lines and "gags."

The four led a terrible life; they spent the morning and the afternoon in bed sleeping and didn't go to sleep again till dawn.

"We're like cats," La Mell would say. "We hunt at night and sleep by day."

La Mell, La Goya, La Rabanitos and Engracia would go at night to the centre of Madrid, accompanied by a white-bearded beggar with a smiling face and a striped cap.

The old man came to beg alms; he was a neighbour of the girls and they called him Uncle Tarrillo, bantering him upon his frequent sprees. He was utterly daft and loved to talk upon the corruption of popular manners.

La Mell said that Uncle Tarrillo had tried, one night after they had returned alone from the Jardinillos del Deposito de Agua, to violate her and that he had made her laugh so much that it was impossible.

The mendicant would wax indignant at the tale and would pursue the indiscreet maid with all the ardour of an old faun.

Of the four girls the ugliest was La Mell; with her big, deformed head, her black eyes, her wide mouth and broken teeth, her dumpy figure, she looked like the lady-jester of some ancient princess. She had been on the point of becoming a chorus-girl; she was balked, however, for despite her good voice and excellent ear for music, she could not pronounce the words clearly because of her missing teeth.

La Mell was always in high spirits, singing and laughing at all hours of the day and night. She carried in her apron-pocket a tiny powder-puff with a mirror on the inside of the cover; she would stop at every other step to gaze at herself by the light of a street-lantern and powder her face.

She was affectionate and kind-hearted. Her excessive ugliness made Manuel gag. The lass was eager to win him but Vidal advised his cousin not to take up with her; La Goya suited him better, for she made more money.

La Mell was not at all to Manuel's taste, despite her affectionate caresses; but La Goya was compromised with El Soldadito, a man with a position, as she said, for when he went to work he turned the crank of an handorgan.

This organ-grinder took all the receipts of La Goya, who, as the prettiest of the quartet, enjoyed the most numerous patronage; El Soldadito watched her and when she went off with anybody, followed, waiting for her to come out of the house of assignation so that he could collect her earnings.

Vidal, of the four, condescended to choose La Rabanitos and Engracia as the objects of his protection; the two girls were forever disputing over him. La Rabanitos looked like a pocket-edition of a woman; a white little face with blue streaks about her nose and her mouth; a rachetic, wizened body; thin lips and large eyes of schlerotic blue; she dressed like an old woman, with her sombre little cloak and her black dress; such was La Rabanitos. She was bothered with frequent hemorrhages; she spoke with all the mannerisms of a granny, making queer twists and turns, and she spent all her spare change on dry salt tunny fish, caramels and other dainties.

Engracia, Vidal's other favourite, was the typical brothel inmate: her face was white with rice powder; her dark, flashing eyes had an expression of purely animal melancholy; as she spoke she showed her blue teeth, which contrasted with the whiteness of her powdered countenance. She leaped from joy to dejection without transition. She could not smile. Her face was as soon darkened by stupidity as it was illuminated by a ribald merriment, insulting and cynical.

Engracia had little to say and when she spoke it was to utter something particularly bestial and filthy, of involved cynicism and pornography. Her imagination was of monstrous fertility.

A macabrous sculptor might have hit upon a work of genius by cutting the thoughts of this girl into the stone representing some infernal Dance of Death.

Engracia could not read. She wore loud waists, blue and pink; a white kerchief on her head and a coloured apron; she trotted along with a swaying movement, so that the coins in her purse kept jingling. She had been eight years in this brothel life, and was only sixteen in all. She was sorry to have grown up, for she said that she had earned far more as a little girl.

The friendship of Manuel and Vidal with these girls lasted a couple of months; Manuel could not make up his mind to take up with La Mella; she was too repulsive; Vidal widened the horizons of his activity, tippled with a gang of *chulos* and devoted himself to the conquest of a flower-girl who sold carnations.

Engracia and La Rabanitos conceived a violent hatred for the lass.

"That strumpet?" La Rabanitos would say. "Why, she's already as disreputable as us...."

One night Vidal did not put in his usual appearance at Casa Blanca, and two or three days later he showed up at the Puerta del Sol with a tall, buxom woman garbed in grey.

"Who's that?" asked Manuel of his cousin.

"Her name's Violeta; I've taken up with her."

"And the other one, at Casa Blanca?"

Vidal shrugged his shoulders.

"You can have her if you wish," he said.

Vidal's former sweetheart likewise disappeared from Casa Blanca and, after he had been unable to collect the two weeks' rent, the administrator put Manuel out into the street and sold the furnishings: a few empty bottles, a stew-pot and a bed.

For several days Manuel slept upon the benches of the Plaza de Oriente and on the chairs of La Castellana and Recoletos. It was getting toward the end of summer and he could still sleep in the open. A few cntimos that he earned by carrying valises from the stations helped him to exist, though badly, until October.

160

There were days when the only thing he ate was the cabbage stalks that he picked up in the marketplaces; other days, on the contrary, he treated himself to seventy-eight cntimo banquets in the chop-houses.

October came around and Manuel began to feel cold at night; his eldest sister gave him a frayed overcoat and a muffler; but despite these, whenever he could find no roof to shelter him he almost froze to death in the street.

One night in the early part of November Manuel stumbled against El Bizco at the entrance to a caf on La Cabecera del Rastro; the cross-eyed ragamuffin was bent over, almost naked, his arms crossed against his chest, barefoot; he presented a painful picture of poverty and cold.

Dolores La Escandalosa had left him for another.

"Where can we go to sleep?" Manuel asked him.

"Let's try the caves of La Montaa," answered El Bizco.

"But can we get in there?"

"Yes, if there aren't too many."

"Come on, then."

The two crossed through the Puerta de Moros and Mancebos Street to the Viaduct; they traversed the Plaza de Oriente, following along Bailen and Ferraz Streets, and, as they reached the Montaa del Prncipe Po, ascended a narrow path bordered by recently planted pines.

El Bizco and Manuel went along in the dark from one side to the other, exploring the hollows of the mountain, until a ray of light issuing from a crevice in the earth betrayed one of the caves.

They approached the hole; from within came the interrupted hum of hoarse voices.

By the flickering light of a candle which was held in position on the ground by two rocks, more than a dozen outcasts, some seated and some on their knees, formed a knot of card-players. In the corners might be discerned the hazy outlines of men stretched out on the sand.

A fetid vapour was exhaled by the cave.

The flame flickered, illuminating now a corner of the den, now the pale face of one of the players, and as the light blinked, the shadows of the men grew long or short on the sandy walls. From time to time was heard a curse or a blasphemy.

Manuel thought that he had beheld something like this before in one of his feverish nightmares.

"I'm not going in," he said to El Bizco.

"Why?" asked his companion.

"I'd rather freeze."

"As you please, then. I know one of these fellows. He's El Interprete."

"And who is this Interprete?"

"The captain of all the mountain vagabonds."

Despite these assurances Manuel hesitated.

"Who's there?" came a voice from inside.

"I," answered El Bizco.

Manuel dashed off at full speed. Near the cave stood a group of two or three huts, with a yard in the middle, surrounded by a rough stone wall.

This, according to the ironic name given to it by the ragamuffins, was the Crystal Palace, the nest of some low-flying turtledoves who frequented the Montaa barracks and who, at night, were joined by friendly hawks and gerfalcons.

The entrance to the yard was closed by a double-panelled door.

Manuel examined it to see if it yielded, but it was strong, and was armoured with tins that were stretched out and nailed down upon mats.

He thought that nobody could be there and tried to climb the wall; he scaled the low rubble inclosure and as he advanced, got caught in a wire; a stone fell noisily from the wall, a dog began to bark furiously, and a curse echoed from inside.

Manuel, convinced that the nest was not empty, took to flight. He sought shelter in a doorway that was somewhat protected from the rain and huddled down to sleep.

It was still night when he awoke shivering with the cold, trembling from head to foot. He started to run so as to warm himself; he reached the Paseo de Rosales and strode up and down several times.

It seemed that the night would never end.

The rain ceased; the sun came out in the morning; Manuel took refuge in a hollow on the slope of the embankment. The sun began to warm him most deliciously. Manuel dreamed of a very white, exceedingly beautiful woman with golden tresses. Frozen almost to death, he drew near the lady, and she wrapped him in her golden strands and he nestled tenderly, ever so tenderly in her lap....

CHAPTER VI

Seor Custodio and His Establishment—The Free Life.

... And he was in the midst of the most ravishing dreams when a harsh voice recalled him to the bitter, impure realities of existence.

"What are you doing there, loafer?" some one was asking him.

"I!" mumbled Manuel, opening his eyes and staring at his questioner. "I'm not doing anything."

"Yes, I can see that. I can see that."

Manuel got up; before him he beheld an old man with greyish hair and gloomy mien, with a sack across his shoulder and a hook in his hand. The fellow wore a fur cap, a sort of yellowish overcoat and a reddish muffler rolled around his neck.

"Have you a home?" asked the man.

"No, sir."

"And you sleep in the open?"

"Well, as I haven't any home...."

The ragpicker began to rake over the ground, fished up some objects and various papers, shoved them into the sack and turning his gaze again upon Manuel, added:

"You'd be better off if you went to work."

"If I had work, I'd work; but I haven't, so ..."—and Manuel, wearied of these useless words, huddled into his corner to continue his slumbers.

"See here," said the ragdealer, "you come along with me. I need a boy ... I'll feed you."

Manuel looked at the man without replying.

"Well, do you want to or not? Hurry up and decide."

Manuel lazily arose. The rag man, sack slung across his shoulder, climbed the slope of the embankment until he reached Rosales Street, where he had a cart drawn by two donkeys. The man told them to move on and they ambled down toward the

164

Paseo de la Florida, thence through Virgen del Puerto Avenue to the Ronda de Segovia. The cart, with its license plate and number, was a tumbledown affair, held together by strips of brass, and was laden with two or three sacks, buckets and baskets.

The ragman, Seor Custodio,—that was what he gave as his name,—looked like a good-natured soul.

From time to time he would bend over, pick up something from the street and throw it into the cart.

Underneath the cart, attached to it by a chain, jogged along in leisurely fashion a dog with yellowish locks, long and lustrous,—an amiable creature who appeared to Manuel as good a canine as his master was a human being.

* * * * *

Between the Segovia and Toledo bridges, not far from the head of Imperial Avenue, there opens a dark depression with a cluster of two or three squalid, wretched huts. It is a quadrangular ditch, blackened by smoke and coal dust, hemmed in by crumbling walls and heaps of rubbish.

As he reached the edge of this depression, the rag-dealer stopped and pointed out to Manuel a hovel standing next to a broken-down merry-go-round and some swings, saying:

"That's my house; take the cart down there and unload it. Can you do that?"

"Yes, I think so."

"Are you hungry?"

"Yes, sir."

"Very well. Then tell my wife to give you a bite."

Manuel accompanied the cart into the hollow over an embankment of rubbish. The ragdealer's house was the largest in the vicinity and had a yard as well as an adjoining shed.

Manuel stopped before the door of the hut; an old woman came out to meet him.

"What do you want, kid?" she asked. "Who sent you here?"

"Seor Custodio. He told me to ask you where to put the stuff that's in the cart."

The woman pointed out the shed.

"He told me also," added the boy, "to say that you should give me something to eat."

"I know you, you foxy creature," mumbled the old woman. And after grumbling for a long time and waiting for Manuel to dump out the contents of the cart, she gave him a slice of bread and a piece of cheese.

The woman unharnessed the two mules and released the dog, who began to bark and play with contentment; he snapped playfully at the mules, one black and the other a silvery grey, who turned their eyes upon him and showed their teeth; desperately he gave chase to a white cat with a tail that bristled like a feather-duster, then approached Manuel, who, seated in the sun, was nibbling at his bit of cheese and his slice of bread, waiting for something. They both had lunch.

Manuel walked around the dwelling and looked it over. One of its narrow sides was composed of two bathing-houses.

These two bathing-houses were not joined, but left between them a space filled in by a rusty iron door such as is used to fasten shops.

The two longer walls of the ragdealer's hovel were formed of stakes paid with pitch, and the wall opposite to that built of the bathing-houses was constructed of thick, irregular rocks and curved outward with a swelling like that of a church presbytery. Within, this curve corresponded to a hollow in the manner of a wide vaulted niche occupied by the hearth.

The house, despite its tiny size, had no uniform system of roofing; in some spots tiles were substituted by strips of tin with heavy rocks holding them in place and the interstices chinked with straw; in others, the slate was mortared together with mud; in still others, sheets of zinc provided protection.

The construction of the house betrayed each phase of its growth. As the shell of the tortoise augments with the development of the reptile, so did the rag-dealer's hovel little by little increase. At first it must have been a place for only one person, something like a shepherd's hut; then it widened, grew longer, divided into rooms, afterwards adding its annexes, its shed and its yard.

Before the door to the dwelling, on a flat stretch of tamped earth, stood a carrousel surrounded by a low, octagonal impalement; the stakes, decayed by the action of moisture and heat, still showed a vestige of their original blue paint.

Those poor merry-go-round steeds, painted red, offered to the gaze of the indifferent spectator the most comical, and at the same time the most pathetic sight. One of the coursers was of indeterminate hue; the other must have forgotten his paws in his mad race; one of them, in a most elegantly uncomfortable pose, symbolized humble sadness and honest, refined modesty.

At the side of the merry-go-round rose a frame formed of two tripods upon which rested a beam, whose hooks served as the support of swings.

The black ditch harboured three other hovels, all three constructed of tins, rubbish, planks, ruins and other similar building materials. One of the shacks, owing either to old age or deficient architecture, threatened to collapse, and the owner, no doubt, had sought to prevent its fall by sinking a row of stakes along one of the walls, against which it leaned like a lame man upon his crutch; another house flaunted like a flagstaff a long stick on its roof with a pot stuck on the top....

After eating Manuel informed the old woman that Seor Custodio had told him he might remain there.

"Tell me whether there's anything else for me to do," he concluded.

"All right. Stay here. Take care of the fire. If the pot boils, let it; if it doesn't, throw a bit of coal into the flames. Reverte! Reverte!" shouted the woman to the dog. "Let him remain here."

She went off and Manuel was left alone with the dog. The stew boiled merrily. Manuel, followed by Reverte, made an inspection tour of the house. It was divided into three compartments: a tiny kitchen and a large room into which the light entered through two high, small windows.

In this room or store-room, on all sides, from the walls and from the ceiling, hung old wares of various hue, white clothes, red boinas and Catalonian caps, strips of crape cloaks. On the shelves and on the floor, separated according to class and size, were flasks, bottles, jars, canisters, a veritable army of glass and porcelain pots; the ranks were broken by those huge, green, dropsical pharmacy bottles, and several heavy-paunched demi-johns; then came half-gallon bottles, tall and dark; straw-covered vases; this was followed by the section devoted to medicinal waters, the most varied and numerous of all, for it included Seltzer-water siphons, oxygenized-water siphons, bottles of gaseous water, Vichy, Mondariz, Carabana; after this came the small fry, the perfume phials, the pots, the cold-cream jars, the cosmetic receptacles.

In addition to this department of bottles there were others: canned-goods tins and pans ranged on shelves; buttons and keys kept in chests; remnants, ribbons and laces rolled around spools or cardboard.

All this struck Manuel as quite pleasant. Everything was in its proper place, relatively spick and span; the hand of a methodical, neat person was in evidence.

167

In the kitchen, which was kalsomined, shone the few scullery utensils. On the hearth, above the white ashes, an earthenware stew-pot was boiling away with a gentle purring.

From outside there scarcely came the distant noises of the city, which filtered in like a pale sound; it was as quiet as in a remote hamlet; now and then a dog would bark, some cart would creak as it bumped along the road, then silence would be restored and in the kitchen nothing would be heard save the *glu glu* of the pot, like a soft, confidential murmur....

Manuel cast a look of satisfaction through the chink of the door to the dark ditch outside. In the corral the hens were scratching the earth; a hog was rooting about, running in fright from one side to the other, grunting and quivering with nervous tremours; Reverte was yawning, blinking gravely, and one of the donkeys was wallowing delightedly amidst broken pots, decayed baskets and heaps of refuse, while the other, as if scandalized by such unrefined comportment, contemplated him with the utmost surprise.

All this black earth filled Manuel with an impression of ugliness, yet at the same time with a sense of tranquillity and shelter; it seemed a proper setting for him. This soil formed the daily deposits of the dumping-place; this earth, whose sole products were old sardine-cans, oyster shells, broken combs and shattered pots; this earth, black and barren, composed of the detritus of civilization, of bits of lime and mortar and factory refuse, of all that the city had cast off as useless, seemed to Manuel a place made especially for him, for he himself was a bit of the flotsam and jetsam likewise cast adrift by the life of the city.

Manuel had seen no other fields than the sad, rocky meadows of Soria and the still sadder ones of the Madrilenian suburbs. He did not suspect that in spots uncultivated by man there were green meadows, leafy woods, beds of flowers; he thought that trees and flowers were born only in the gardens of the rich....

Manuel's first days in Seor Custodio's house seemed too burdened; but as there is plenty of free roaming in the ragdealer's life, he soon grew accustomed to it.

Seor Custodio arose when it was still night, woke Manuel, and they both harnessed the two donkeys to the cart and took the direction to Madrid, on their daily hunt for the old boot and the discarded tatter. Sometimes they went by way of Melanclicos Avenue; others, by the Rondas or through Segovia Street.

Winter was coming on; at the hour when they sallied forth Madrid was in complete darkness. The ragdealer had his fixed itinerary and his schedule of call stations. When he went by way of the Rondas and drove up Toledo Street, which was his most frequent route, he would halt at the Plaza de la Cebada and the Puerta de Moros, fill his hamper with vegetables and continue toward the heart of the city.

168

On other days he travelled through Melanclicos Avenue to the Virgen del Puerto, from here to La Florida, then to Rosales Street, where he rummaged in the rubbish deposited by the tip-carts, continuing to the Plaza de San Marcial and arriving at the Plaza de los Mostenses.

On the way Seor Custodio let nothing escape his eye; he would examine it and keep it if it were worth the trouble. The leaves of vegetables went into the hampers; rags, paper and bones went into the sacks; the half-burned coke and coal found a place in a bucket and dung was thrown into the back of the cart.

Manuel and the ragdealer returned early in the morning; they unloaded the cart on the flat earth before the door, and husband, wife and the boy would separate and classify the day's collection. The rag-dealer and his wife were amazingly skilful and quick at this work.

On rainy days the assorting was done in the shed. During such weather the depression became a dismal, repellant swamp, and in order to cross it one had to sink into the mud, in places half way up to the knee. Everything would drip water; the hog in the yard would wallow in mire; the hens would appear with their wings all black and the dog scampered about coated with mud to the ears.

After the sorting of the collection, Seor Custodio and Manuel, each with a basket, would wait for the dump-carts to arrive, and as the refuse was tipped out, they would set about sorting it on the very dumping-grounds: pasteboard, rags, glass and bones.

In the afternoon Seor Custodio would go to certain stables in the Argelles district to clean out the manure and take it to the orchards on the Manzanares.

Between one thing and another Seor Custodio made enough to live in a certain comfort; he had a firm grasp upon his business and as he was under no compulsion to sell his wares promptly, he would wait for the most opportune occasion so that he could sell with advantage.

The paper that he thus stored up was purchased by the pasteboard factories; they gave him from thirty or forty cntimos per arroba. The manufacturers required the paper to be perfectly dry, and Seor Custodio dried it in the sun. As they tried at times to get the best of him in weight, he used to place in each sack two or three full arrobas, weighed with a steelyard; on the cloth of the sack he would inscribe a number in ink, indicating the amount of arrobas it contained, and these sacks he held in a sort of cellar or ship's hold that he had dug into the ground of the shed.

When there was a great quantity of paper he sold it to a pasteboard factory on Acacias Avenue. Seor Custodio's journey was not in vain, for in addition to selling the goods at a fancy price, he would, on the way back, drive his cart in the direction of a pitch factory of the vicinity, and there he picked up from the ground a very fine coal that burned excellently and gave as much heat as slag.

He sold the bottles to wine houses, to liquor and beer distilleries; the medicine flasks he disposed of to pharmacists; the bones went to the refineries and the rags to the paper factories.

The bread leavings, vegetable leaves and fruit cores were reserved for the feed of the pigs and hens, and what was of no use at all was cast into the rotting-place, converted into manure and sold to the orchards near the river.

On the first Sunday that Manuel spent there, Seor Custodio and his wife took the afternoon off. For many a day they had never gone out together because they were afraid to leave the house alone; this day they dressed up in their best and went on a visit to their daughter, who worked as a modiste in a relative's shop.

Manuel was glad to be left by himself with Reverte, contemplating the house, the yard, the ditch; he turned the carrousel round and it creaked ill-humouredly; he climbed up the swing frame, looked down at the hens, teased the pig a little and then ran up and down with the dog chasing after him barking merrily in feigned fury.

This dark depression attracted Manuel somehow or other, with its rubbish heaps, its gloomy hovels, its comical, dismantled merry-go-round, its swings, and its ground that held so many surprises, for a rough, ordinary pot burgeoned from its depths as easily as a lady's elegant perfume phial; the rubber bulb of a prosaic syringe grew side by side with the satin, scented sheet of a love letter.

This rough, humble life, sustained by the detritus of a refined, vicious existence; this almost savage career in the suburbs of a metropolis, filled Manuel with enthusiasm. It seemed to him that all the stuff cast aside in scorn by the capital,—the ordure and broken tubs, the old flower-pots and toothless combs, buttons and sardine tins,—all the rubbish thrown aside and spurned by the city, was dignified and purified by contact with the soil.

Manuel thought that if in time he should become the owner of a little house like Seor Custodio's, and of a cart and donkeys, and hens and a dog, and find in addition a woman to love him, he would be one of the almost happy men in this world.

170

CHAPTER VII

Seor Custodio's Ideas—La Justa, El Carnicern, and El Conejo.

Seor Custodio was an intelligent fellow of natural gifts, very observant and quick to take advantage of a situation. He could neither read nor write, yet made notes and kept accounts; with crosses and scratches of his own invention he devised a substitute for writing, at least for the purposes of his own business.

Seor Custodio was exceedingly eager for knowledge, and if it weren't that the notion struck him as ridiculous, he would have set about learning how to read and write. In the afternoon, work done, he would ask Manuel to read the newspapers and the illustrated reviews that he picked up on the streets, and the ragdealer and his wife listened with the utmost attention.

Seor Custodio had, too, several volumes of novels in serial form that had been left behind by his daughter, and Manuel began to read them aloud.

The comment of the ragdealer, who took this fiction for historic truth, was always perspicacious and just, revelatory of an instinct for reasoning and common sense. The man's realistic criticism was not always to Manuel's taste, and at times the boy would make bold to defend a romantic, immoral thesis. Seor Custodio, however, would at once cut him short, refusing to let him continue.

For professional reasons the ragdealer was much preoccupied with thought of the manure that went to waste in Madrid. He would say to Manuel:

"Can you imagine how much money all the refuse that comes from Madrid is worth?"

"No."

"Then figure it out. At seventy cntimos per arroba, the millions of arrobas that it must amount to in a year.... Spread this over the suburbs and have the waters of the Manzanares and the Lozoya irrigating all these lands, and you'd see a world of gardens and orchards everywhere."

Another of the fellow's fixed ideas was that of reclaiming used material. It seemed to him that lime and sand could be extracted from mortar refuse, live plaster from old, dead plaster, and he imagined that this reclamation would yield a huge sum of money.

Seor Custodio, who had been born near the very depression in which his house was situated, felt for his particular district, and for Madrid in general, a deep enthusiasm; the Manzanares, to him, was as considerable a river as the Amazon.

Seor Custodio had two children, of whom Manuel knew only Juan, a tall, swarthy sport who was married to the daughter of a laundry proprietress in La Bombilla. The ragdealer's daughter, Justa by name, was a modiste in a shop.

During the first few weeks neither of the children came to their parents' home. Juan lived in the laundry and Justa with a relative of hers who owned a workshop.

Manuel, who spent many hours in conversation with Seor Custodio, noted very soon that the rag-dealer, though fully aware of his very humble condition, was a man of extraordinary pride and that as regarded honour and virtue he had the ideas of a mediaeval nobleman.

One Sunday, after he had been living there a month Manuel had finished his meal and was standing at the door when he saw a girl with her skirts gathered come running down the slope of the dumping-ground. As she approached and he got a close look at her, Manuel went red and then blanched. It was the lass that had come two or three times to the lodging-house to fit the Baroness's dresses; but she had since then grown to womanhood.

She drew near, raising her skirt and her starched petticoats, careful not to soil her patent-leather slippers.

"What can she be coming here for?" Manuel asked himself.

"Is father in?" she inquired.

Seor Custodio came out and embraced her. She was the ragdealer's daughter of whom Manuel was forever hearing and whom, without knowing just why, he had imagined as a very thin, emaciated, disagreeable creature.

Justa walked into the kitchen and after looking over the chairs, to see whether there was anything on them that might soil her clothes, she sat down upon one of them. She began to pour forth a flood of unceasing chatter and roared at her own jokes.

Manuel listened without a word; to tell the truth she wasn't quite so good-looking as he had imagined, but she didn't please him any the less for that. She might be about eighteen, was brunette, rather short, with very dark, flashing eyes, a tilted, pert nose, a sensual mouth and thick lips. She was, too, a bit full behind and in the breasts and the hips; she was neat, fresh, with a very high top-knot and a pair of brand-new, polished slippers.

As Justa gabbled on, to the ecstasy of her parents, there came into the kitchen a hump-backed fellow from one of the neighbouring hovels; he was called El Conejo (the rabbit) and his face really showed a great resemblance to the amiable rodent whose name he bore.

172

El Conejo was a member of Seor Custodio's fraternity and knew Justa since she had been a child; Manuel used to see him every day, but never paid any attention to him.

The Rabbit walked into Seor Custodio's and began to talk nonsense, laughing in violent outbursts, but in so mechanical a manner that it provoked his hearers, for it seemed that behind this continuous laughter lay a very deep bitterness. Justa touched his hump, for, as is known, this brings good luck, whereupon El Conejo exploded with merriment.

"Have you been lugged up again before the chief?" she asked.

"Oh, yes. Often ... hee-hee ..."

"What for?"

"Because the other day I started to shout in the street: 'Bargains! Who'll buy Sagasta's umbrella, Kruger's hat, the Pope's urinal, a syringe lost by a nun while she was talking with the sacristan! ...'"

El Conejo trumpeted this at the top of his lungs and Justa held her sides with laughter.

"And don't you sing mass any more the way you used to?"

"Oh, sure."

"Let's hear it, then."

The humpback had taken for his scandalous parody, the Preface of the Mass, and for the sacred words he substituted others with which he announced his business. He began to bellow:

"Who will sell me any ... slippers ... pants ... hempen sandals ... old shoes ... secondhand clothes ... syringes ... urinals and even chemises."

The hunchback's cries made Justa laugh nervously. El Conejo, after repeating the Preface several times took up the melody of the rogations and sang some strains in a high soprano, others in a basso profundo:

"The high silk-hat" ... and instead of saying *Libranos domine*, he went on: "I'll buy for spot cash.... Your old vest ... will fetch a five-peseta piece...."

Then he had to stop to let Justa laugh.

She was not slow in perceiving that she had attracted Manuel, and despite the fact that he seemed no great conquest to her, she became serious, egged him on and glanced at him furtively with looks that sent the boy's blood pounding faster.

After the ragdealer's daughter had left, Manuel felt as if he had been abandoned to darkness. He thought that he could live for two or three weeks on her incendiary glances alone.

The next day, when Manuel met El Conejo he listened to the nonsense that the hunchback spoke, with his eternal harping on the Bishop of Madrid-Alcal, and then tried to shift the conversation toward the topic of Seor Custodio and his family.

"Justa's a pretty girl, isn't she?"

"Psch ... yes," and El Conejo looked at Manuel with the reserved mien of a person concealing a mystery.

"You've known her since she was a kid, haven't you?"

"Yes. But I've known plenty of other girls, too."

"Has she a sweetheart?"

"She must have. Every woman has a sweetheart unless she's mighty ugly."

"And who is Justa's fellow?"

"Anyone; I shouldn't be surprised if it were the Bishop of Madrid-Alcal."

El Conejo was a very intelligent looking person; he had a long face, a curved nose, a broad forehead, tiny, sparkling eyes and a reddish beard that tapered to a point, like a goat's.

A peculiar tic, a convulsive twitch of the nose, would agitate his face from time to time, and it was this that completed his resemblance to a rabbit. His merriment was just as likely to find issue in a nervous, metallic, sonorous outburst as in a muffled, clownish guffaw. He would stare at people from top to bottom and from bottom to top in a manner all the more insolent for its jesting character, and to add to the mockery he would detain his gaze upon his interlocutor's buttons, and his eyes would dance from the cravat to the trousers and from the boots to the hat. He took special care to dress in the most ridiculous fashion and he liked to adorn his cap with bright cock feathers, strut about in riding boots and commit similar follies.

174

He was fond, too, of confusing folks with his lies, and so firmly did he state the tales of his own invention that it was hard to tell whether he was fooling or speaking in all seriousness.

"Haven't you heard what happened this afternoon to the Bishop of Madrid-Alcal over at Las Cambroneras?" he would say to some acquaintance.

"Why, no."

"Sure. He was on a visit bringing alms to Garibaldi and Garibaldi gave the Bishop a cup of chocolate. The Bishop sat down, took a sip, when zip! ... Nobody knows just what happened; he dropped dead."

"Why, man! ..."

"It's the Republicans that are behind it all," affirmed El Conejo in his most serious manner, and he would be off to another place to spread the news or perpetrate another hoax. He would join a group.

"Have you heard what happened to Weyler?"

"No. What was it?"

"Oh, nothing. On his return from camp some flies attacked his face and ate up a whole ear. He went across Segovia bridge bleeding terribly."

This was how the buffoon managed to enjoy himself.

Mornings he would sling his sack over his shoulder and proceed to the centre of Madrid where he shouted his business through the thoroughfares, mingling his cries with the names of political leaders and famous men,—a habit that had won him more than once the honour of appearing before the police-chief's desk.

El Conejo was as perverse and malevolent as a demon; any maiden in the vicinity that was going around with a secret bundle might well tremble lest he surprise her. He knew everything, he scented it out; apparently, however, he took no mean advantage of his discoveries. He was content to scare folks out of their wits.

"El Conejo must know," was the regular response when anything was suspected.

"I don't know a thing; I've seen nothing," he would answer, laughing. "I don't know anything." And that was all anybody could get out of him.

As Manuel got to know El Conejo better he felt for him, if not esteem, at least a certain respect because of his intelligence.

This ragman jester was so cunning that often he deceived his colleagues of El Rastro, who were far from being a set of fools.

Almost every morning the ragdealers would forgather at the head of El Rastro, to exchange impressions and used articles. El Conejo would learn beforehand just what was needed by the stand merchants, and he would buy the articles of the rag men, selling them in turn to the merchants; between this bartering and selling he always came out the gainer....

During the Sundays that followed, Justa amused herself by working upon Manuel's feelings. The girl was absolutely free in her talk and had a thorough, finished knowledge of all the Madrilenian phrases and wiles.

At first Manuel acted very respectfully; but seeing that she took no offence he grew gradually more daring and ventured so far as to steal embraces. Justa easily freed herself and would laugh at sight of the fellow's serious countenance and his glance ablaze with desire.

With the licentious manner that characterized her, Justa would carry on scabrous conversations, telling Manuel what men said to her on the street and the proposals that they whispered into her ears; she spoke with especial delight of shopmates who had lost their virginal bloom in La Bombilla or Las Ventas with some Don Juan of the counter who spent his days twirling his mustache before the mirror of a perfumery or silk shop.

Justa's words were always freighted with a double meaning and were, at times, burning allusions. Her mischievous manner, her flaunting, unbridled coquetry, scattered about her an atmosphere of lust.

Manuel felt a painful eagerness to possess her, mingled with a great sadness and even hatred, when he saw that Justa was making sport of him. Many a time when he saw her come Manuel vowed to himself not to speak a word to her, not to look at her or say anything; then she would hunt him out and tease him by beckoning to him and touching his foot.

Justa's temper was disconcertingly uneven. Sometimes when Manuel clasped her about the waist and sat her down on his knees, she would let him squeeze her and kiss her all he pleased; at others, however, simply because he had drawn near and taken her by the hand, she would give him such a hard slap that his senses whirled.

"And come back for more," she would add, seemingly indignant.

Manuel would feel like crying with anger and rage, and would have to contain himself lest he blurt out, with childish logic: "Why did you let me kiss you the other afternoon?" But at once he saw how ridiculous such a question would seem.

176

Justa got to feel a certain liking for Manuel, but it was a sisterly, a friendly affection; he never appealed to her seriously as a sweetheart or a suitor.

This flirtation, which to Justa was a mere sham of love, constituted for Manuel a painful awakening from puberty. He had dizzy attacks of passionate desire which left him mortally weak and crushed. Then he would stride along hurriedly with the irregular gait of one suffering from locomotor ataxia; many a time, crossing the pine grove of the Canal, he was seized with an impulse to jump into the river and drown himself. The filthy black water, however, hardly invited to immersion.

It was during these libidinous spells that dark, sinister thoughts assailed him,—the notion of how useless his life was, the certainty of an adverse fate,—and as he considered the vagabond, abandoned existence that awaited him, his soul walked with bitterness and sobs rose in his throat....

One winter Sunday Justa, who had got into the habit of visiting her parents on every holiday, did not appear. Manuel wondered whether the inclement weather might be the cause and he spent the whole week restless and nervous, counting the days that would intervene before their next meeting.

On the following Sunday Manuel went to the corner of the Paseo de los Pontones to wait for the girl to come along; as he espied her at a distance his heart gave a jump. She was accompanied by a young dandy, half bull-fighter and half gentleman, wearing a Cordovan hat and a blue cloak covered with embroidery. At the end of the avenue Justa took leave of her escort.

The next Sunday Justa carne to her parents' home with a girl friend and the young man of the embroidered cloak; she introduced the young man to Seor Custodio. Afterward she said that he was the son of a butcher from La Corredera Alta, and to her mother Justa confessed bashfully that the gentleman had asked permission to pay her attentions. This phrase pay attentions, which is spoken by the haughtiest princess and the humblest janitress with equally lingering pleasure, enchanted the ragdealer's wife, particularly as the gentleman in question came of a wealthy family.

In Seor Custodio's home the butcher's son was considered as the paragon of all perfections and beauties; Manuel alone protested and El Carnicerin (the little butcher),—as he had named him derisively from the very first moment,—was the object of his murderous glances.

When Manuel understood that Justa considered the butcher's son as an ideal suitor, his sufferings were cruel. It was no longer melancholy that moved his soul, which was now agitated by the most raging despair.

The fellow had too many advantages over him: he was tall, graceful, slender, flaunted a fair, budding moustache, was well-dressed, his fingers covered with rings, an expert dancer and skilful player on the guitar; he almost had a right to be as content with himself as he was.

"How can that woman fail to see," thought Manuel, "that the fellow loves only himself? While I...."

On Sundays there used to be dancing on a lawn near the Ronda de Segovia, and Seor Custodio, with his wife, Justa and her sweetheart, would go there. They would leave Manuel behind to watch the house, but at times he would run off to see the dance.

When he caught sight of Justa dancing with El Carnicerin he was overwhelmed with a desire to drown them both.

The suitor, moreover, was a terrible show-off; he would affect a feminine grace as he danced, and it seemed as if he were applauding and complimenting himself. He kept so finically true to the rhythm of the dance that a spontaneous motion might ruin everything. He wouldn't have officiated at mass with greater ceremony.

As was natural, such a complete knowledge of the science of dancing, united to his consciousness of superiority, endowed El Carnicern with admirable self-possession. It was he who was permitting himself indolently to be won by Justa, who was frantically fond of him. As they danced she threw herself upon him, her eyes sparkled and her nostrils dilated; it seemed as if she wished to dominate him, swallow him, devour him. She did not take her eyes off him, and if she saw him with another woman her face at once turned colour.

One afternoon El Carnicern was speaking to a friend. Manuel drew near so as to overhear the conversation.

"Is that the girl?" his friend inquired.

"She's the one."

"Boy, maybe she isn't daffy over you."

And El Carnicern, with a conceited smile, added:

"I've turned her head, all right."

Manuel could have torn out the fop's heart at that moment.

His disappointment in love made him think of leaving Seor Custodio's house.

One day he met, near the Segovia bridge, El Bizco and another ragamuffin that was with him.

They were both in tatters; El Bizco looked grimmer and more brutish than ever. He wore an old jacket through the rents of which peered his dark skin; according to what they said, they were both on their way to the intersection of Aravaca road and the Extremadura cart-road, to a spot they called the Confessionary. They expected to meet El Cura and El Hospiciano there and rob a house.

"What do you say? Will you join us?" asked El Bizco sarcastically.

"No, I won't."

"Where are you now?"

"In a house ... working."

"There's a brave fool for you! Come on, join us."

"No. I can't.... Listen, how about Vidal? Didn't you ever see him again?"

El Bizco's face turned grimmer than ever.

"I'll get even with that scoundrel. He won't escape before I carve a nice scar on his face.... But are you coming along with us or not?"

"No."

Seor Custodio's ideas had worked a strong influence upon Manuel; but since, despite this, his adventurous instincts persisted, he thought of going off to America, or becoming a sailor, or something of that sort.

CHAPTER VIII

The Square—A Wedding in La Bombilla—The Asphalt Caldrons.

The betrothal of El Carnicern and Justa was formally arranged, Seor Custodio and his wife bathed in rose water, and only Manuel believed that in the end the wedding would never take place.

El Carnicern was all together too haughty and too much of a fine fellow to marry the daughter of a ragdealer; Manuel imagined that now the butcher's son would try to take advantage of his opportunity. But for the present nothing authorized such malevolent suppositions.

El Carnicern was generosity itself and showed delicate attentions to his sweetheart's parents.

One summer day he invited the whole family and Manuel to a bull fight. Justa dressed up very fetchingly in her best to make a worthy companion to her lover. Seor Custodio took out his finest apparel: the new fedora, new although it was more than thirty years old; his coat of doubled cloth, excellent for the boreal regions, and a cane with a horn handle, bought in El Rastro; the ragdealer's wife wore a flowered kerchief, while Manuel made a most ridiculous appearance in a hat that was taken from the shop and protruded about a palm's length before his eyes, a winter suit that suffocated him and a pair of tight shoes.

Behind Justa and El Carnicern, Seor Custodio, his wife and Manuel attracted everybody's attention and left a wake of laughter.

Justa turned back to look at them and could not help smiling. Manuel walked along in a rage, stifling, his hat pressing tightly against his forehead and his feet aching.

They got into a street car at Toledo Street and rode to the Puerta del Sol; there they boarded art omnibus, which took them to the bull ring.

They entered and, guided by El Carnicern, sat themselves down in their respective places. The spectacle had begun and the amphitheatre was packed. Tier upon tier was crammed with a black mass of humanity.

Manuel glared into the arena; they were about to kill the bull near the stone wall that bounded the ring, at a short distance from where they were. The poor beast, half dead already, was dragging himself slowly along, followed by three or four toreros and the matador, who, curved forward, with his red flag in one hand and his sword in the other, came behind. The matador was scared out of his wits; he stood before the bull, considered carefully just where he was to strike him, and at the beast's slightest movement he prepared to escape. Then, if the bull remained quiet a while, he struck him once, again, and the animal lowered his head; with his tongue hanging out,

180

dripping blood, he gazed out of the sad eyes of a dying creature. After much effort the matador gave him the final stroke and killed him.

The crowd applauded and the band blared forth. The whole business struck Manuel as pretty disagreeable, but he waited eagerly. The mules came out and dragged off the dead bull.

Soon the music ceased and another bull appeared. The picadores remained close to the walls while the toreros ventured a bit nearer to the beast and waved their red flags, at once rushing back.

This was hardly anything like the picture Manuel had conjured up for himself, or like what he had seen in the coloured illustrations of *La Lidia*. He had always imagined that the toreros, in the sheer skill of their art, would play around with the bull, and there wasn't any of this; they entrusted their salvation to their legs, just like the rest of the world.

After the inciting tactics of the toreros, two *monosabios* began to beat a picador's horse with several sticks, until they got him to advance as far as the middle of the arena. Manuel had a close view of the horse; he was a large, white, bony creature with the saddest look on his face. The _>monosabios_ goaded him on toward the bull. Soon the beast drew near, the picador pricked him with the point of his lance, the bull lowered his head for the attack and threw the horse into the air. The rider fell to the ground and was picked up in a trice; the horse tried to raise himself, with his intestines sprawling on the sand in a pool of blood; he trampled on them with his hoofs, his legs wavered and he fell convulsively to the ground.

Manuel arose deathly pale.

A *monosabio* approached the horse, who was still quivering; the animal raised his head as if to ask help, whereupon the man stabbed him to death with a poniard.

"I'm going. This is too nasty for anything," said Manuel to Seor Custodio. But it was no easy matter to leave the ring at that moment.

"The boy," said the ragdealer to his wife, "doesn't like it."

Justa, who had learned what was the matter, burst into laughter.

Manuel waited for the bull to be put to death; he kept his eyes fixed downward; the mules came out again, and as they dragged off the horse's body the intestines were left on the ground until a monosabio came along and dragged them off with a rake.

"Look at that tripe!" cried Justa, laughing.

Manuel, without a word, and unmindful of the eyes that were turned his way, left the tier. He went down to a series of long galleries, ranged with vile-smelling urinals, and tried unsuccessfully to locate the exit.

He was filled with rage against the whole world, against the others and against himself. The spectacle seemed to him a most repugnant, cowardly atrocity.

He had imagined bull-fighting to be something utterly distinct from what he had just witnessed; he had thought that always it would display the mastery of man over beast, and that the sword-thrusts would flash like lightning; that every moment of the struggle would bring forth something interesting and suggestive; and instead of a spectacle such as he had visioned, instead of a gory apotheosis of valour and strength, he beheld a petty, filthy thing, a medley of cowardice and intestines, a celebration in which one saw nothing but the torero's fear and the cowardly cruelty of the public taking pleasure in the throb of that fear.

"'This," thought Manuel, "could please only folks like El Carnicerin, effeminate loafers and indecent women."

Reaching home Manuel ragingly threw down his hat, pulled off his shoes and got out of the suit in which he had so ridiculously gone to the bull fight....

Manuel's indignation elicited plenty of comment from Seor Custodio and his wife, and he himself was somewhat intimidated by it; he understood that the spectacle hadn't been to his taste; what struck him as strange was that it should rouse so much anger, such rage in him.

Summer went by; Justa began to make preparations for her wedding, and in the meantime Manuel thought of leaving Seor Custodio's house and getting out of Madrid altogether. Whither? He didn't know; the farther away, the better, he thought.

In November one of Justa's shopmates got married, in La Bombilla, Seor Custodio and his wife found it impossible to attend, so that Manuel accompanied Justa.

The bride lived in the Ronda de Toledo, and her house was the meeting-place for all the guests.

At the door a large omnibus was waiting; it could hold any number of persons.

All the guests piled in; Justa and Manuel found a place on the top and waited a while. The bride and bridegroom appeared amidst a throng of gamins who were shouting at the top of their lungs; the groom looked like a dry goods clerk; she, emaciated and ugly, looked like a monkey; the best man and the bridesmaids followed after, and in this group a fat old lady, flat-nosed, cross-eyed, white-haired, with a red rose in her hair and a guitar in her hand, advanced with a *flamenco* air.

182

"Hurrah for the bride and groom! Hurrah for the best man and the maid-of-honour!" shouted the cross-eyed fright; there was a chorus of unenthusiastic responses and the coach departed amidst a hubbub and a shouting. On the way everybody shrieked and sang.

Manuel did not dare to rejoice at his failure to see El Carnicern in the crowd; he felt positive that the fellow would show up at Los Viveros.

It was a beautiful, humid morning; the trees, copper-hued, were losing their yellow leaves in the gentle gusts; white clouds furrowed the pale sky, the road glittered with the moisture; afar in the fields burned heaps of dead leaves and thick curls of smoke rolled along close to the soil.

The coach halted before one of the inns of Los Viveros; everybody rolled out of the omnibus and the shouts and clamouring were heard anew. El Carnicern was not there, but he soon appeared and sat down at table right beside Justa.

The day seemed hateful to Manuel; there were moments in which he felt like crying. He spent the whole afternoon despairing in a corner, watching Justa dance with her sweetheart in time to the tunes of a barrel-organ.

At night Manuel went over to Justa and with comic gravity, said to her abruptly:

"Come along, you—" and seeing that she paid no attention to him, he added, "Listen, Justa, let's be going home."

"Get away. Leave me in peace!" she retorted rudely.

"Your father told you to be back home by night. Come along, now."

"See here, my child," interposed El Carnicern with calm deliberation. "Who gave you a taper to bear at this funeral?"

"I was entrusted to...."

"All right. Shut up. Understand?"

"I don't feel like it."

"Well, I'll make you with a good ear-warming."

"You make me? ... Why, you're nothing but a low-down lout, a thief—" and Manuel was advancing against El Carnicern, when one of the fellow's friends gave him a punch in the head that stunned him. The boy made another attempt to rush upon the butcher's son; two or three guests pushed him out of the way and shoved him out on to the road at the door of the inn.

"Starveling! ... Loafer!" shouted Manuel.

"You're one yourself," cried one of Justa's friends tauntingly after him. "Rabble! Guttersnipe!"

Manuel, filled with shame and thirsting for vengeance, still half dazed by the blow, thrust his cap down over his face and stamped along the road weeping with rage. Soon after he left he heard somebody running toward him from behind.

"Manuel, Manolillo," said Justa to him in an affectionate, jesting voice. "What's the matter?"

Manuel breathed heavily and a long sigh of grief escaped him.

"What's the matter? Come, let's return. We'll go together."

"No, no; go away from me."

He was at a loss; without another word he set off on a run toward Madrid.

The wild flight dried his tears and rekindled his fury. He meant not to return to Seor Custodio's even if he died of hunger.

His rage rose in waves up his throat; he felt a blind madness, hazy notions of attacking, of destroying everything, of razing the world to the ground and disemboweling every living creature.

Mentally he promised El Carnicern that if ever he met him alone, he would sink his claws into his neck and strangle him; he would split the fellow's head in two as they do to hogs, and would hang him up head downwards with a stick between his ribs and another in his intestines, and moreover, he'd place a tin box at his mouth into which his cursed pig's blood could drip.

Then he generalized his hatred and considered that society itself was against him, intent only upon plaguing him and denying him everything.

Very well, then; he would go against society, he would join El Bizco and assassinate right and left, and when, wearied of committing so many crimes, he would be led to the scaffold, he would look scornfully down from the platform upon the people below and die with a supreme gesture of hatred and disdain.

184

While all these thoughts of wholesale extermination thronged in his brain, night was falling. Manuel walked up to the Plaza de Oriente and followed thence along Arenal Street.

A strip of the Puerta del Sol was being asphalted; ten or twelve furnaces ranged in a row were belching thick acrid smoke through their chimneys. The white illumination of the arc-lights had not yet been turned on; the silhouettes of a number of men who were stirring with long shovels the mass of asphalt in the caldrons danced diabolically up and down before the flaming mouths of the furnaces.

Manuel approached one of the caldrons when suddenly he heard his name called. It was El Bizco; he was seated upon some paving blocks.

"What are you doing here?" Manuel asked him.

"We've been thrown out of the caves," answered El Bizco, "and it's cold. What about you? Have you left the house?"

"Yes."

"Have a seat."

Manuel sat down and rested his back against a keg of asphalt.

Lights began to sparkle in the balconies of the residences and in the shop windows; the street cars arrived gently, as if they were vessels floating in, with their yellow, green and red lanterns; their bells rang and they traced graceful circles around the Puerta del Sol. Carriages, horses, carts came rattling by; the itinerant hawkers cried their wares from their sidewalk stands; there was a deafening din.... At the end of one street, against the coppery splendour of the dusk stood out the tapering outlines of a belfry.

"And don't you ever see Vidal?" asked Manuel.

"No. See here, Have you got any money?" blurted El Bizco.

"Twenty or thirty cntimos at most."

"Fine."

Manuel bought a loaf of bread, which he gave to El Bizco, and the two drank a glass of brandy in a tavern. Then they went wandering about the streets and, at about eleven, returned to the Puerta del Sol.

Around the asphalt caldrons had gathered knots of men and tattered gamins; some were sleeping with their heads bent against the furnace as if they were about to attack it in bull fashion. The ragamuffins were talking and shouting, and they laughed at the passers-by who came over out of curiosity for a closer look.

"We sleep just as if we were in the open country," said one of the idlers.

"It wouldn't be at all bad," added another, "to take a walk now over to the Plaza Mayor and see whether they wouldn't give us a pound of ham."

"It has trichinae in it, anyway."

"Take care of that spring-matress," bellowed a flat-nosed gamin who was going about striking the sleepers with a stick in the shins. "Hey, there, you're rumpling the sheets!"

At Manuel's side, a rachetic urchin with thick lips and streaked eyes and one of his feet bandaged in dirty rags, was crying and groaning; Manuel, engrossed in his own thoughts, had not noticed him before.

"Some howling you're doing," came to the sufferer from a boy who was stretched out on the ground with his legs cramped close to his chest and his head pillowed against a rock.

"It hurts like anything."

"Then shut up, grin and bear it. Hang yourself."

Manuel thought that he heard El Carnicern's voice and glanced toward the speaker. The fellow's hat was pulled down over his eyes and his face was not visible.

"Who's that?" asked Manuel of El Bizco.

"He's the captain of the cave gang: El Interprete."

"And what's he talking to the kid like that for?"

El Bizco shrugged his shoulders with a gesture of indifference.

"What's' the trouble?" Manuel inquired of the boy.

"I have a wound in my foot," replied the child, bursting again into tears.

186

"Shut up, I tell you," interrupted El Interprete, aiming a kick at the sufferer, who managed to escape the blow. "Go tell your troubles to your bitch of a mother.... Damn it all! It's impossible to sleep here."

"Then to hell with you!" shouted Manuel.

"Who are you talking to?" demanded El Interprete, shoving his cap back on his head and revealing a brutish face with a flat nose and high cheekbones.

"To you, you thief, you coward!"

El Interprete sprang to his feet and strode over to Manuel, who, in an excess of fury seized him with both hands by the neck, kicked him in the leg with his right heel, made him lose his balance and threw him to the ground. There he thumped him violently. El Interprete, more muscular than Manuel, was able to get to his feet again; but he had lost his nerve and Manuel, gathering strength from his anger, threw him down a second time and was about to crash a rock into his face when a pair of municipal guards happened along and kicked them apart. El Interprete went off disgraced.

The members of the crowd calmed down and went off, one after the other, to resume their positions around the caldron.

Manuel sat down upon some paving blocks; the struggle had wiped out the memory of the blow he had received that afternoon; he felt brave and in a jesting mood, so, facing the curiosity-hunters that were watching the group, some laughing and others eyeing the urchins with pity, he addressed them.

"The session is about to close," he said. "Now we shall begin the community singing lessons. We're about to commence snoring, ladies and gentlemen. Let the public have no fear. We'll take good care of the bedsheets. Tomorrow we'll send them to the river to be washed. Now is the time. Whoever so desires," and he pointed to a rock, "may take advantage of these pillows. They're excellent pillows, such as are used by the Marquises of Archipipi. Whoever doesn't wish to sleep on them, let him be gone and not bother us. Ea! Gentlemen! If you don't pay I'll summon the servant and tell her to close...."

"It's the same with all of them," said one of the ragamuffins. "They talk nonsense when they get sleepy. They all look as if they were starved."

Manuel felt as garrulous as a mountebank. When he had wearied, he leaned against a heap of stones and with arms crossed prepared to sleep.

Shortly after this the group of curiosity-hunters had dispersed; only a guard and an old gentleman were left, and they discussed the ragamuffins in tones of pity.

The gentleman deplored the way these children were abandoned and said that in other countries they built schools and asylums and a thousand other things. The guard shook his head dubiously. At last he summed up the conversation, saying in the tranquil manner of a Galician:

"Take my word for it: there's no good left in any of them."

Manuel, hearing this, began to tremble; he arose from his place on the ground, left the Puerta del Sol and began to wander aimlessly about.

"There's no good left in any of them!" The remark had made a deep impression upon him. Why wasn't he good? Why? He examined his life. He wasn't bad, he had harmed nobody. He hated El Carnicern because that fellow had robbed him of happiness, had made it impossible for him to go on living in the one corner where he had found some affection and shelter. Then contradicting himself, he imagined that perhaps he was bad after all, and in this case the most he could do was to reform and become better.

Absorbed in these reflections, he was passing along Alcal Street when he heard his name called several times. It was La Mell and La Rabanitos, skulking in a doorway.

"What do you want?" he asked.

"Nothing, man. Just a word with you. Have you come into your money yet?"

"No. What are you doing?"

"Hiding here," answered La Mell.

"Why, what's the trouble?"

"There's a round-up, and that skunk of an inspector wants to take us to the station, even if we do pay him. Keep us company!"

Manuel accompanied them for a while; but they both picked up a couple of men on the way and he was left alone. He returned to the Puerta del Sol.

The night seemed to him endless; he walked around and walked yet again; the electric lights were extinguished, the street-cars stopped running, the square was left in darkness.

Between Montera and Alcal Streets there was a caf before whose illuminated windows women passed up and down dressed in bright clothes and wearing crape kerchiefs, singing, accosting benighted passers-by; several loafers, lurking behind the lanterns, watched them and chatted with them, giving them orders....

188

Then came a procession of street-women, touts and procurers. All of parasitical, indolent, gay Madrid issued forth at these hours from the taverns, the dens, the gambling-houses, the dives and vice resorts, and amidst the poverty and misery that throbbed in the thoroughfares these night-owls strutted by with their lighted cigars, conversing, laughing, joking with the prostitutes, indifferent to the agony of all these ragged, hungry, shelterless wretches who, shivering with the cold, sought refuge in the doorways.

A few old strumpets remained at the street-corners, wrapped in their cloaks, smoking....

It was long before the heavens grew bright; it was still night when the coffee stands were opened, and the coachmen and ragamuffins went up for their cup or glass. The gas lamps were extinguished.

The light from the watchmen's lanterns danced across the grey pavement, which already was dimly lighted by the pale glow of dawn, and the black silhouettes of the ragdealers stood out against the heaps of ordure as they bent over to take the rubbish. Now and then some pale benighted fellow with his coat collar raised, would glide by as sinister as an owl before the growing light and soon some workmen passed.... Industrious, honest; Madrid was preparing for its hard daily task.

This transition from the feverish turmoil of night to the calm, serene activity of morning plunged Manuel into profound thought.

He understood that the existence of the night-owls and that of the working folk were parallel lives that never for an instant met. For the ones, pleasure, vice, the night; for the others, labour, fatigue, the sun. And it seemed to him, too, that he should belong to the second class, to the folk who toil in the sun, not to those who dally in the shadows.

END OF "TO BUSCA,"

(THE QUEST)

The second volume of the trilogy is called "Mala Hierba" (Weeds); the third, "Aurora Roja" (Red Dawn).

Printed in Great Britain
by Amazon.co.uk, Ltd.,
Marston Gate.